TENNESSEE WILLIAMS

Cat on a Hot Tin Roof

with commentary and notes by
PHILIP C. KOLIN

Advisory Editor
MATTHEW ROUDANÉ

METHUEN DRAMA

Methuen Drama Student Edition

10 9 8 7 6 5 4 3 2 1

This edition first published in the United Kingdom in 2010 by
Methuen Drama
A & C Black Publishers Ltd
36 Soho Square
London W1D 3QY
www.methuendrama.com

By special arrangement with The University of the South, Sewanee, Tennessee

The Dylan Thomas epigraph is from Dylan Thomas,
'Do not Go Gentle into that Good Night', *The Collected Poems*, Dent, 1952

A CIP catalogue record for this book is available from the British Library

ISBN 978 1 408 11439 1

Typeset by Country Setting, Kingsdown, Kent CT14 8ES
Printed and bound in Great Britain by CPI Cox & Wyman, Reading RG1 8EX

Contents

Tennessee Williams: 1911–1983   v

Plot   xi

Commentary   xvi
   Cat and the plantation mythos   xvi
   Cat and America in the 1950s   xx
   Versions of *Cat on a Hot Tin Roof*   xxiv
   Structure   xxv
   Language   xxvi
   Characters   xxxi
   Production history   xlix
   Adaptations of *Cat* for film and TV   lx

Further Reading   lxv

CAT ON A HOT TIN ROOF   1

'Author and Director'   117

Notes   122

Questions for Further Study   126

Tennessee Williams: 1911–83

1908   Williams's sister, Rose Isabelle, is born 19 November in Columbus, Mississippi.

1911   Thomas Lanier Williams III is born on 26 March in Columbus, Mississippi.

1911   Rose, Tom, and their mother, Edwina Dakin Williams,
–18   live with Edwina's parents, the Reverend Walter Dakin, an Episcopal priest, and his wife Rosina Otte Dakin, chiefly in Clarksdale, while father Cornelius Coffin Williams works as a travelling salesman.

1918   Williams's younger brother, Walter Dakin, born on 21 February; the Williams family moves to St Louis where father becomes a branch manager at the International Shoe Company.

1926   After only one semester at Soldan High School in St Louis, Williams transfers to University City High School.

1928   Publishes the first story for which he is paid – 'The Vengeance of Nitrosis' – in *Weird Tales*. Goes on a European trip with his maternal grandfather.

1929   In September, Williams enters the University of Missouri and joins Alpha Tau Omega fraternity. In October the stock market crashes resulting in the Great Depression.

1932   Williams's father withdraws him from the University of Missouri for failing ROTC (Reserve Officers Training Course) and starts him as a clerk at the International Shoe Company, a job he loathes.

1935   First production of Williams's one-act play – *Cairo! Shanghai! Bombay!* – by Memphis Garden Players, a group of amateur actors.

1936   In January, Williams enrols at Washington University in St Louis and writes the one-act play *Twenty-Seven Wagons Full of Cotton*.

1937   Writes a full-length, leftist play, *Candles to the Sun*, about
        a coal-mine strike, staged by the Mummers (amateur
        group of actors) in St Louis. Rose is committed to
        Farmington (Missouri) State Mental Hospital; Williams
        is heartbroken and feels tremendous guilt.

1937   Studies playwriting at the University of Iowa with
 −39   Edward Charles Mabie, nicknamed 'the Boss';
        Mummers stage *Fugitive Kind*. Graduates from Iowa
        with a BA in English. Writes another leftist play, *Not
        About Nightingales*, about a prison riot in Pennsylvania.
        Becomes a vagabond, travelling to New Orleans where
        he possibly has his first homosexual experience in the
        French Quarter.

1939   Meets Audry Wood, his agent for over thirty years.
        Signs his name Tennessee Williams for the first time in
        a short story 'Field of Blue Children' in *Story Magazine*.
        Receives a $100 prize in a competition organised by
        the Group Theatre (where Elia Kazan's wife, Molly
        Day Thacher, is one of the readers) for his collection
        of one-act plays *American Blues*. Wins a grant of $1,000
        from the Rockefeller Foundation.

1940   Studies playwriting with John Gassner and Erwin
        Piscator at the New School for Social Research. His
        first professional production of a play − *The Battle of
        Angels* − has a disastrous Boston tryout on 30 December
        but closes on 11 January 1941 after the City Council
        protests about its sexual content.

1941   Travels around the country, writing one-act plays,
 −42   stories, and poems; visits Key West for the first time;
        has the first of his four cataract operations.
        Collaborates on *You Touched Me!* with Donald Windham.
        Meets Jordan Massee, Sr, a model for Big Daddy.

1943   Works for Metro-Goldwyn-Mayer (MGM) on a
        screenplay *The Gentleman Caller* (later *The Glass Menagerie*)
        but is fired after only six months. Rose has a prefrontal
        lobotomy, leaving her mentally challenged for life; the
        operation is referenced in *Suddenly Last Summer*.

1944   National Institute for Arts and Letters awards Williams
        $1,000 for *Battle of Angels*. Margo Jones, theatre founder

and longtime friend, directs the one-act play *The Purification* at the Pasadena Playhouse in California. *The Glass Menagerie* premieres in Chicago on 26 December.

1945   *The Glass Menagerie*, Williams's first big success, runs for 561 performances on Broadway, winning the New York Drama Critics' Circle Award and the Donaldson Award. He publishes thirteen one-act plays in *Twenty-Seven Wagons Full of Cotton*.

1947   *A Streetcar Named Desire*, directed by Elia Kazan, opens on 3 December at the Barrymore Theatre on Broadway and runs for 855 performances, spawning two road companies. Williams meets his longtime companion and lover Frank Merlo (1929–63), a US Navy veteran.

1948   Alfred Kinsey's *Sexual Behavior in the Human Male* is
 –49   published on 3 January 1948. *Streetcar* wins the triple crown of the Pulitzer, New York Drama Critics' Circle Award, and the Donaldson Award. It premieres across the world (e.g., Mexico, Belgium, France, Germany, Sweden). British premiere of *Streetcar* (Sept.) directed by Laurence Olivier, starring wife Vivien Leigh. *One Arm and Other Stories*, a collection of sexually explicit stories, is published. *Summer and Smoke* opens on Broadway.

1950   First (and worst according to Williams) film adaptation of *The Glass Menagerie* released by Warner Brothers. The novel *The Roman Spring of Mrs Stone* is published.

1951   *The Rose Tattoo* opens in New York for 306 performances. Warner Brothers releases film of *Streetcar*, also directed by Kazan and designed by Jo Mielziner; produced by Irene Selznick, former wife of David O. Selznik, producer of *Gone with the Wind*.

1952   *Streetcar* wins National Film Critics' Circle Award. Williams is elected to the National Institute of Arts and Letters. Publishes the story 'Three Players of a Summer Game', the genesis of *Cat on a Hot Tin Roof*.

1953   *Camino Real*, with gay characters and themes, opens on Broadway.

1954   *Hard Candy* (another collection of explicit fiction) is published. Works on drafts of *Cat on a Hot Tin Roof*. Kazan insists on major revisions.

1955   *Cat on a Hot Tin Roof* premieres on 24 March on
       Broadway and runs for 649 performances, winning
       Williams his second Pulitzer Prize and third New York
       Drama Critics' Circle Award; film of *The Rose Tattoo*
       released; Reverend Walter Dakin dies, aged ninety-
       seven.

1956   *Baby Doll* screenplay condemned for sexual content by
       the Catholic Church. *Cat on a Hot Tin Roof* opens in
       Paris (16 December); it is banned in Ireland. First book
       of poetry, *In the Winter of Cities*, is published.

1957   *Orpheus Descending* (revision of *Battle of Angels*) closes in
       New York after 68 performances. Cornelius Coffin
       Williams dies.

1958   Film version of *Cat on a Hot Tin Roof* is released by
       MGM, directed and co-written by Richard Brooks; it is
       Williams's biggest box-office hit; *Suddenly Last Summer*
       opens Off-Broadway. British premiere of *Cat on a Hot
       Tin Roof* using Williams's original third act is staged at
       a private club because of ban by Lord Chamberlain.

1959   *Sweet Bird of Youth*, with antagonist Boss Finley, opens
       for 95 performances on Broadway. Screen version of
       Suddenly Last Summer is released.

1960   Williams's comedy, *Period of Adjustment*, opens in New
       York for 132 performances. Film of *Orpheus Descending*,
       set in a hellish Delta, opens under the title of *Fugitive
       Kind*.

1961   Williams's last Broadway success, *The Night of the Iguana*,
       wins the New York Drama Critics' Circle Award and
       runs for 316 performances. Film versions of *Summer and
       Smoke* and *The Roman Spring of Mrs Stone* come out.

1962   Films of *Sweet Bird of Youth* (starring Paul Newman and
       Geraldine Page) and *Period of Adjustment* (starring Jane
       Fonda) are produced.

1963   *The Milk Train Doesn't Stop Here Anymore* opens on
       Broadway. Frank Merlo dies of lung cancer.

1964   Film of *The Night of the Iguana* is released, starring
       Richard Burton as a drunken clergyman.

1966   *Slapstick Tragedy* (*The Mutilated* and *The Gnadiges Fraulein*)
       closes after only seven performances.

1967   First version of *The Two-Character Play*, about a brother and sister, opens in London.

1968   *The Seven Descents of Myrtle* (later entitled *Kingdom of Earth*) opens on Broadway for 27 performances; contains graphic sex scene.

1969   *In the Bar of a Tokyo Hotel* premieres 11 May in New York for 23 performances. Williams is committed to psychiatric unit of Barnes Hospital, St Louis, 27–8 June. The Stonewall (named after the gay bar) Riots erupt in New York City, marking the start of the Gay Liberation movement. Williams is baptised a Roman Catholic in Key West.

1970   *Dragon Country: A Book of Plays* is published. Williams appears on the *David Frost Show* and for the first time publicly admits his homosexuality.

1971   *Out Cry* (rewritten version of *The Two-Character Play*) opens on 2 July in Chicago.

1972   *Small Craft Warnings* moves to Broadway for 200 performances; Williams plays the role of Doc, a drunken, disbarred physician, the only time he acts in a professional production of his plays.

1974   *Eight Mortal Ladies: A Book of Stories* is published. *Cat on a Hot Tin Roof* opens at the American Shakespeare Festival Theatre, Stratford, CT, with Williams's final, new third act.

1975   Williams given the Medal of Honor for Literature by the National Arts Club. *Memoirs* published, as well as a novel, *Moise and the World of Reason*. *Red Devil Battery Sign*, occasioned by Watergate, is staged in Boston and New York. First Broadway revival of *Cat on a Hot Tin Roof* with Williams's final script.

1976   *Eccentricities of a Nightingale* (revision of *Summer and Smoke*) premieres in New York.

1977   *Vieux Carré* closes after only 11 performances. Second book of poetry, *Androgyne, Mon Amour*, published. First televised *Cat on a Hot Tin Roof*.

1978   *A Lovely Sunday for Crève Coeur* opens in New York for 36 performances.

1979   Receives Presidential Arts Achievement Award.

1980   President Jimmy Carter presents Williams with Medal of Freedom. Edwina Dakin Williams dies at the age of ninety-five. *Clothes for a Summer Hotel*, about Zelda Fitzgerald's madness, opens.

1981   *Something Cloudy, Something Clear* opens Off-Broadway; last of Williams's plays to be professionally produced while he was alive.

1983   Williams dies on 24 February in New York at the Hotel Elysée (Elysian Fields, the 'Land of the Happy Dead' in *Streetcar*) after choking on a medicine-bottle cap.

1984   Showtime (cable TV) airs *Cat on a Hot Tin Roof*, re-shown on PBS TV in 1985.

1985   Tennessee Williams's *Collected Stories* is published.

1988   British revival of *Cat on a Hot Tin Roof*, directed by Howard Davies, uses Williams's original script (1955), the first production of the play in Britain in thirty years.

1990   Davies directs *Cat on a Hot Tin Roof* for its Broadway revival.

1996   Rose Williams dies on 5 September at the age of eighty-eight.

1998   *Not About Nightingales* premieres at London's Royal National Theatre. Written in 1938, the play was rediscovered in the 1980s by Vanessa Redgrave. Corin Redgrave stars as warden Boss Whalen.

2004   Williams Revival at the Kennedy Center.

2005   *Mister Paradise and Other One-Act Plays*, including thirteen previously unpublished one-acts, is released.

2008   Dakin Williams dies on 20 May. *The Traveling Companion and Other Plays* (twelve previously uncollected experimental plays) is published. First professional production of *Cat on a Hot Tin Roof* with a black cast on Broadway (comes to London in 2009).

Plot

Cat opens with the physical symbols Williams uses to develop his characters. Coming out of the bathroom, after freshening up from a disgustingly messy dinner with Gooper's 'no-neck' children, Maggie stands in front of a mirror and a dressing table. Showering and powdering are part of her repertoire to entice Brick back to bed and continue to be alluring to Big Daddy. The mirror reflects her identity, and Brick's too. 'Who are you?' she says in front of it (30). She is worried that Brick's older brother Gooper and his obnoxious wife Mae will cut Brick and her out of Big Daddy's inheritance. They never let Big Daddy and Big Mama forget that Maggie is childless and that Brick is a drunkard. Branding Mae's repulsive children as 'no-neck monsters', she tries to thwart Gooper and Mae's plot to disinherit Brick and her.

Brick is symbolised throughout the play by his crutch, his liquor cabinet, and his pyjamas. He needs the crutch because of a broken ankle he suffered jumping hurdles on the athletic field at his old high school at 3 a.m. In every act, he hobbles and falls on stage. Dressed in silk pyjamas, he is a patient in his own isolated world/ward. When Maggie informs him that 'Now we know that Big Daddy's dyin' of *cancer*', all he can say is, 'Do we?' His terse replies to her – 'Did you *say* something', or 'How about that' (9–10) – show that he is disconnected, emotionally and physically, from his wife as well as from his father. Refusing to communicate or sleep with Maggie, and drowning himself in liquor, Brick wants to escape the pain and the obligation of self-disclosure. He drinks until he hears the 'click', the silence that brings him peace. The empty bed in the middle of the room, another key prop, is an accusing reminder of Maggie and Brick's childless, loveless marriage. Wanting no part of family life, Brick refuses to even sign a card or play a part in giving Big Daddy the birthday present Maggie has bought. The white silk pyjamas Maggie asks Brick to wear parallel the soft cashmere robe she buys for Big Daddy. In the midst of Maggie's litany of hurts, Sister Woman, Mae, barges in, berating Brick and Maggie. Attempting to convince her meddling sister-in-law that Brick is a loyal husband, Maggie talks about a hunting trip that she and Brick plan to make very soon to Moon Lake. When Big Mama bursts in, overjoyed by the news that Big Daddy does not have cancer, she also attacks Maggie for not having children and for having a husband who drinks. Disgusted, Big Mama leaves the room.

Quick-witted and tenacious, Maggie quickly recovers from Big Mama's inquisitorial intrusion to return to her attempted conversation with Brick. Hoping to coax him into bed, she informs him that other men find her attractive, including Big Daddy whom she likes and admires, and reveals that a man tried to pick her up recently. Even though the mirror in the bedroom reflects a beautiful, desirable wife, Brick refuses to see Maggie or himself clearly in it. Wanting her out of his life, he encourages Maggie to 'take a lover', but she refuses because it would lead to a divorce. She vows to take care of Brick, but he rejects everyone's help, especially hers. Maggie is determined that they will not lose Brick's inheritance; after an impoverished childhood she could not bear to be poor again. Standing in front of the mirror, she sighs folornly, 'I'm dressed, all dressed, nothing else for me to do' (35), while Brick whistles 'vaguely' at her, another sign of his cool estrangement.

But Brick's apathy turns to anger when she mentions his relationship with his deceased friend Skipper. When Maggie declares that love-making with Brick 'didn't just peter out in the usual ways, it was cut off short long before the natural time for it to' (30), she summarises what has happened and forecasts confrontations to come. Nothing thus far has brought Brick's emotions to the surface as much as Maggie's reference to 'the truth about that thing with Skipper' (35). *Cat* gives us several accounts of 'that thing'. In Act Two, we will hear Brick's and Big Daddy's side, but, according to Maggie in Act One, she made love to Skipper to be closer to Brick and to put Skipper on notice that Brick was her husband. But Brick accuses her of smearing that relationship as 'dirty', and blames her for destroying his friendship with Skipper. Maggie protests that she saw their friendship as 'pure'. Confessing that she tried to get Skipper to stop loving her husband, she went to his room one night, but after he was unable to make love, Skipper drank himself to death, for which Brick will never forgive Maggie. At the end of Act One, Dixie, one of Gooper's unmannerly brood, barges into the bedroom, taunting Brick and Maggie once more. Linking birth and death, Act One ends with the family gathering in Brick's room to celebrate Big Daddy's sixty-fifth birthday.

Act Two
Act Two, with Big Daddy's long-awaited entrance, might be divided into three parts. In the first part, Big Daddy responds to the uninvited guests in Brick's bedroom. Like his son, he has little tolerance for his family and only contempt for his wife Ida, who brings in *'an enormous birthday cake ablaze with candles'* (44). Given Big Daddy's real medical condition, ordering Ida to blow out the candles is painfully ironic. As in Act One, Brick evades contact and conversation by leaving the room, going back and forth to the bar, and refusing to answer direct questions with direct answers. Big Daddy's interrogations begin with wanting to know why Brick is crippled, which triggers talk about his son's sexual identity. Brick's character has been besmirched by Gooper and Mae because of their disgusting eavesdropping, and an angry Big Daddy orders them out of Brick's bedroom, another in a series of evictions in *Cat*.

In the second part of Act Two, Big Daddy demands to know why Brick does not sleep with Maggie. Big Daddy asserts that 'the human animal is a beast' because he tries to win immortality through accumulating possessions. He then describes his trips to Europe where Big Mama tried to purchase everything in sight and to Africa where a woman made her young daughter solicit him. Just as Brick repulses Maggie's lovemaking, Big Daddy rejects his wife's. But for all of Big Daddy's power he cannot communicate with his son, who blames his father for talking in circles. Brick finally confesses that he drinks because of 'disgust', a response which sparks a father–son confrontation over lies and corruption. Brick complains, though, that he never lied to his father, and Big Daddy likewise responds, 'Then there is at least two people that never lied to each other' (75). Sadly, Brick is the only one to tell his father the truth. Yet Brick's disgust translates into mendacity, a subject Big Daddy knows well, having lived in an abhorrent marriage and dealing with the rest of his contentious family. But having received a good bill of health, he orders Brick to straighten up.

In the third part of Act Two, pressuring Brick further, Big Daddy wants to know how and why Skipper died. At the turning point of the play, Big Daddy declares that Brick's relationship with Skipper was 'not exactly normal' (76). Vindictively, Brick intimates that his father was also in a compromised (homosexual) relationship with Jack Straw and Peter Ochello, the old 'bachelors' who many years ago hired Daddy as an overseer on their plantation. But Big Daddy discusses the Straw–Ochello relationship without ever directly answering Brick's charge. Through a fiery volley of words, Brick resents his father's accusation that the relationship with Skipper was 'unnatural', and assures him that he would have spurned Skipper if he were gay. Inquiring, then, why Skipper cracked up, Big Daddy learns that Brick blames Maggie for Skipper's death. But when Big Daddy insists that something has been left out of his son's story, Brick confesses that one night Skipper called to make 'a drunken confession' (84) but that he hung up on him. Because of Brick's cowardice and self-deception, Big Daddy accuses him of mendacity, translated into 'disgust' with himself for not facing the truth. Amid fireworks celebrating Big Daddy's birthday, Brick inadvertently reveals what everyone but Big Daddy knows – this is his last birthday. He quickly regrets the disclosure and accuses himself of being 'less alive'. The act ends with Big Daddy's harrowing cry condemning all liars.

Act Three

Serving as a bridge between acts, Big Daddy's condemning voice cascades into Act Three as he exits. Unlike the intimately charged conversations in Acts One and Two, the exchanges in Act Three occur when the Pollitt clan/ensemble gather to discuss Big Daddy's medical condition and to break the bad news to Big Mama. Reassured that Big Daddy is all right, judging by the huge meal he has just eaten, Big Mama is nevertheless concerned about this 'mysterious family conference' (138). When the time comes to reveal the truth about this 'black thing' that has invaded the Pollitt house, Dr Baugh vindicates himself by telling Big Mama that Big Daddy's condition has 'gone past the knife' (97). As he has done throughout *Cat*, Brick leaves the room, and even sings a song, sealed in his own pain-proof world. Unscrupulously, Gooper produces a briefcase (a symbol of his mercenary world) containing trustee papers and medical reports and asserts that as a corporation lawyer he can continue to run the estate. Incensed, Big Mama demands that Gooper put the documents away and implores Brick and Maggie to have an heir.

But, as Williams was keen to emphasise, Big Daddy is not dead yet, and coming back briefly on stage, he vows to keep control of his land. Symbolising the turmoil inside the Pollitt family, a storm blows in, Williams's use of what is known as 'pathetic fallacy': nature reflecting human emotions. Big Daddy then tells his famous crude joke about an elephant's erection and how small it was in comparison to a husband's whose wife and children accompany him at the zoo. The joke reaffirms Big Daddy's manhood while his family paints him as dying. To everyone's shock, Maggie announces she is pregnant. Elated, Big Daddy declares she has 'life in her body' (112), then retreats to where he can look at his plantation, leaving Mae and Gooper in Brick's bedroom where they angrily accuse Maggie of lying before leaving outraged. Confronting Brick, Maggie claims she is now the stronger one, hides his liquor, and insists that he sleeps with her 'to make the lie true' if he wants it back. Echoing a line from Big Daddy in Act Two (52), Brick's words, 'Wouldn't it be funny if that was true?' provocatively refer to Maggie's love for him and her hoped-for conception.

Commentary

Like many of Wiliams's plays, *Cat on a Hot Tin Roof* takes place in a highly symbolic setting, one that is steeped in the history and myths of the South. In fact, *Cat* excavates two levels of history – the long tradition of ante- and post-bellum (Southern) customs and their literary expression and the more recent history of the 1950s in American political life, the time when *Cat* was written and first performed.

Cat and the plantation mythos

Cat is inseparable from its Southern plantation setting. The South, especially the Mississippi Delta, exerted a strong influence on Williams's life and work. Stretching from Memphis to Yazoo City, the Mississippi Delta comprises an area of 6,250 square miles of flat land enriched by the alluvial deposits of the Mississippi River which was frequently impoverished by floods, insects, and drought. Growing up in Clarksdale in the Mississippi Delta, just seventy miles south of Memphis, Williams was familiar with the Delta towns and people because he visited them with his maternal grandfather, the Reverend Mr Dakin, whose Episcopal church, St George's, was one of Clarksdale's cultural centres. *Cat* is filled with references to Williams's boyhood South: Big Daddy's sprawling plantation of 28,000 acres is located near Clarksdale; Brick's accident at the high school running track is reported in the *Clarksdale Register*; and Big Daddy eats huge quantities of Delta food, such as 'hoppin' John', 'candied yams', and all ingredients for 'a real country dinner' (90). His most important cash crop is cotton, and to celebrate King Cotton, the Delta held festivals with a cotton queen, also alluded to in *Cat*. Although Clarksdale was known for the blues, there are, unfortunately, no references to this musical form (as in *Baby Doll* or *Orpheus*

Descending), but a saxophonist played a Louis Armstrong score before each act in the production of *Cat* in 2008 with an all-black cast.

With its large cotton plantations and the wealthy families that owned them, the Delta was enshrined in the mythos of the nostalgic, antebellum South, the land of valiant courtiers and fair ladies in the spirit of *Gone with the Wind*. Plantation life was often idealised as idyllic and heroic, the aristocratic world of the Wilkes and O'Haras who controlled huge estates such as Twin Oaks and Tara. Planters were portrayed as cultured gentlemen, educated, refined. Their columned houses – such as Longwood – were modelled on classical architecture. The plantation economy was rooted in cotton and harvested by field hands, chattel slaves, whose labour sustained the fictions created about a genteel way of life. Masters and their male heirs adhered to a strict code of chivalry where women were idealised, and business deals were transacted with honour. Plantation life also was noted for its hospitality and romance. Many nineteenth- and twentieth-century plantation novels centred on love affairs amid the magnolias and azaleas. It is this world that *Cat*'s setting evokes.

Yet, despite his Southern roots, Williams replaced the nostalgia of the Old South and its sophisticated planters and elegant rituals with a crass, menacing new South. Big Daddy, the master, is a 'Mississippi redneck' (33) who rode 'a yellow dog freight car' and lived in 'hobo jungles' (78). His daughters-in-law, Maggie and Mae, also come from dirt-poor backgrounds. As Maggie confesses: 'Always had to suck up to people I couldn't stand because they had money and I was poor as Job's turkey' (34). But Mae still pretends she descends from the gentry. Debunking the beauty queen ethos of the South, Maggie satirises the ritual of the cotton queen who would 'sit on a brass throne on a tacky float an' ride down Main Street, smilin', bowin', and blowin' kisses to all the trash on the street' (13). She further recounts how one cotton queen, Susie McPheeter, was riding in a parade when 'some old drunk' in front of the Gayoso Hotel 'shot out a squirt of tobacco juice right in [her] face' (13). Disdaining the world of debutantes, Maggie wore a 'hand-me-down from a snotty rich cousin' (34). Hardly attractive or ladylike, Big Mama looks like a 'Japanese wrestler' (25). And Brick is no dashing, romantic cavalier protecting his lady's honour; twice he tries to hit Maggie with his crutch, once even hurling it at her (39).

Yet Big Daddy's South contains all the comfortable conventions – the setting, quaint, bizarre characters, black servants, and sensational events – that Broadway audiences expected to see and could approve of. The Pollitt plantation with its colourful and crude patriarch, his life-threatening sickness and wealthy estate, the bitter family feud over the inheritance, Brick's alcoholism, secrets from the past, and a steamy, oppressive climate – these were all part of the literary heritage of the South. But, as Albert J. Devlin convincingly argues, Williams 'cunningly' exploited the conventions of the plantation South to 'obscure' his own scepticism about the Broadway commercial theatre (and its values) as he actually sought its approval to secure his fame. Within the historical/ economic context of the plantation South, Williams could express the tensions and anxieties of his own troubled sexual identity through Brick, 'a mirror of [his] artistic identity and his besetting career' (Devlin, 105). Adhering to the nationally acceptable conventions of 'genre, race, class, [and] economy' associated with the South, Williams inserted Brick's (and his own) 'aberrant silence' (Devlin, 104), the 'speechless voice' of a dissident homosexual/playwright who could not openly reveal his 'deepest secrets', his 'mystery'. Williams had thus sown his own failures (the recent commercial disaster of *Camino Real* on Broadway, 1953) into his character besieged with disappointments. According to Devlin, Brick's dilemma reflected, as it disguised, Williams's own 'problematic . . . relations with the Broadway theatre' (107).

Williams also used this symbolic setting to raise questions about and express anxieties over patriarchal control and the rites of inheritance. Traditionally, the economy and hierarchies of plantation life were created and sustained through the power of a patriarch whose legacies exerted control over the land and those who lived on it. A history of the Old South – with its famous plantations – is a history of big daddies, strong-willed men who shaped the world around them. Plantations were passed down from one generation to another through patrilinear succession, fathers to sons, the heirs of heterosexual unions. But, as Michael Bibler argues, *Cat* undermines, even as it sustains, conventional patriarchal control and heterosexuality. For example, Jack Straw and Peter Ochello, the homosexual couple who owned the plantation before Big Daddy, dispel the plantation laws of inheritance through their love affair and their relationship to Big Daddy. In a key speech, he declares:

> I made this place! I was overseer . . . on the old Straw and Ochello plantation. I quit school at ten! I quit school at ten years old and went to work like a nigger in the fields. And I rose to be overseer of the Straw and Ochello plantation. And old Straw died and I was Ochello's partner. (51)

Sexually tolerant, Big Daddy had no qualms about being Ochello's partner and inheriting the plantation. But by admitting that he received the plantation from this gay couple, Big Daddy subverts a heterosexual, patrilinear line of inheritance. Interestingly, no one ever inquires why or how Big Daddy inherited the plantation from Ochello.

Brick also destabilised the plantation mythos. While Blanche loses her ancestral plantation Belle Reve ('Beautiful Dream') in *A Streetcar Named Desire* because of her male ancestor's 'epic fornications', ironically, it is the son, Brick, who risks losing his inheritance by refusing to have an heir with Maggie and because of his ambiguous friendship with Skipper. The conflicts and tensions over Brick's relationship with his wife and with Skipper are more clearly understood in the light of the imperatives of a plantation culture. Like Big Daddy, Brick and Maggie are under the influence of Ochello and Straw. They stay in a *'room that hasn't changed much since it was occupied by the original owners of the place, Jack Straw and Peter Ochello'*. The entire plantation is thus shrunk to this sexually symbolic room. As Bibler again asserts, the shared bedroom 'establishes homosexuality not only as the physical origin of the plantation but also as its metaphysical origin in the loving relationship that "haunts" the room' (384). To Big Daddy, 'it doesn't matter if Brick is homosexual' since 'homosexuality does not destabilize his social position or his masculinity because homosexual desire operates well within plantation hierarchies and codes'. After all, Big Daddy regarded Straw and Ochello as 'double patriarchs' whose lifestyle was not inconsistent with a plantation ethos (395).

Cat and America in the 1950s

America in the 1950s could be termed the age of repression, a time of conformity, insisting that citizens adhere to intensely conservative values. The country was ruled by a staunchly conservative Republican President/General Dwight D. 'Ike' Eisenhower, America's Big Daddy, and his Vice-President, Richard Nixon, whose later presidency (1968–74) scandalised the world by the mendacity of Watergate. In his *Memoirs* (1975), Williams lampooned Nixon for his 'total lack of honesty and . . . moral sense' (95). Big Daddy, too, decries the deceptive language of elected officials: 'Mendacity is one of them five dollar words that cheap politicians throw back and forth' (71). Ike's America was patriotic, heterosexual, and paranoid. America in the 1950s waged a Cold War against Communism, which was demonised as a threat, both from within and outside the country. It was popular, even mandatory, in America to be anti-Communist. A 'Red scare' terrified the country. Fearing a nuclear attack from Russia, America routinely held air-raid drills during which millions of citizens fled to bomb shelters, usually built in their basements, to survive an inevitable nuclear Armageddon.

America's strategy for national defence also lay in vigilantly finding, repelling, and punishing Communists at home. During the 1950s, as never before, the US House and Senate justified taking extraordinary, and sometimes illegal, measures to contain the Communist attack against American family values and national security. To battle the 'Reds' and their 'Pinko' sympathisers, the House on Un-American Activities Committee (HUAC), founded in 1938, and chaired by Senator Joseph McCarthy (Republican, Wisconsin) in the early 1950s, embarked on a notorious witch hunt looking for Communists, especially in entertainment and in the arts. Described as McCarthyism, the HUAC's policy was to search out witnesses to name names and, rather than insisting on hard evidence, accepted and validated lies, innuendo, hearsay, guilt by association, biased informers, and unregulated government eavesdropping. Ten years before *Cat* premiered, Williams had warned America about the dangers of McCarthyism:

> Today we are living in a world which is threatened by totalitarianism. The Fascist and the Communist states have thrown us into a panic of reaction. Reactionary opinion descends like a ton of bricks on the head of any artist who speaks out against the current of prescribed ideas. We are all under wraps of one kind or another, trembling before the spectre of investigation committees . . . ('Something Wild', 46).

Cat satirises and scourges McCarthyism through Gooper's and Mae's despicable, covert actions to gather information about Brick and Maggie to ruin their reputations. Sharing the room next to Brick and Maggie's, they listen through the walls to the couple's conversations, all of which infuriates Big Daddy:

> I hate eavesdroppers, I don't like any kind of sneakin an' spyin' . . . You listen at night like a couple of rutten peekhole spies and go and give a report on what you hear to Big Mama an' she comes to me and says they say such and such and so and so about what they heard goin' on between Brick an' Maggie. (55)

Their reports include information such as 'You won't sleep with her, that you sleep on the sofa' (50). Illustrating their spying, Big Mama and Mae whisper in collusion behind Big Daddy's back (49). Whisper campaigns, eavesdropping, and spying were tactics associated with the HUAC. 'The walls have ears in this place,' warns Big Daddy. Earlier, Maggie asks, 'Hush! Who is out there? Is somebody out there?' (21). Just as Brick's and Maggie's names were sullied in the Pollitt family (allegorised into America, circa 1955), many actors, writers, directors, singers, artists, and musicians were accused

of Communist sympathies and affiliations and blacklisted
from working in Hollywood.

Gays in particular were targeted by policing agencies such
as the HUAC, the FBI, and the military for their supposed
Communist leanings. In 1950, the Republican National
Chairman, Guy Gabrielson, informed his constituents that
'Sexual perverts . . . have infiltrated our Government in recent
years . . . [and they were] perhaps as dangerous as the actual
Communists' (quoted in Paller, 54). It was an easy leap of
(bad) faith to make gays into Communists. According to John
S. Bak, a 'communist suspicion . . . inextricably accompanied
the effete male' (232), branded for being a non-conformist, a
seditious foe of family values, and a threat to national security.
Gays were forced to go underground, stay in the closet, thus
masking their sexual identity. In homophobic America in the
1950s, they were harassed by the police who arrested or
institutionalised them for deviant sexual behaviour. (The
Stonewall Riots, igniting the gay liberation movement in the
summer of 1969, were more than a decade off.) If found out,
gays in the 1950s were fired from their jobs or discharged
from the military. The FBI, led by J. Edgar Hoover, who
history records was himself a closeted gay, conducted intensive
surveillance of gay bars, clubs, and bathhouses to crack down
on this suspicious population. Williams himself was the
subject of FBI and the Department of Navy surveillance for
his sexual contact with sailors during the Second World War
(Mitgang, 122). Being labelled gay was a political crime in
1955.

In such a context, Brick's fear of being branded a
homosexual symbolised a crisis in national identity politics. In
the 1950s, America saw itself as staunchly heteromasculine.
Coming out gay ran the risk of being persecuted as a
Communist, a misfit, the Other, a threat to democracy and
decency. But, as John Bak, Michael Paller, David Savran, and
others have argued, America's identity crisis in the 1950s was
in part triggered by the Kinsey report – *Sexual Behavior in the
Human Male* (1948) – which documented two very troubling
facts: many American men had at least one homosexual
experience and that the enforced dichotomy between gay and

straight was not always clear cut. The destabilisation of gay
and straight identities led to this national anxiety. Brick's
anguish over his sexual identity thus brings this controversy to
the surface by illustrating the homophobia of the times. His
refusal to sleep with Maggie became a tell-tale sign of his
homosexuality for Gooper and Mae. After all, Skipper, who
confessed his love for Brick, could not perform the sexual act
with Maggie. Moreover, Brick's vitriolic homophobic denials
do little to deter the smear campaign against him.

Making sure that they represented an acceptable and
conservative national identity, movies were also policed in
1950s America. Hollywood films were strictly censored by the
PCA (the Production Code Administration), 'the industry's
moral guardian' (Palmer and Bray, 62). To ensure that films
adhered to unsullied, conservative standards, the PCA could
insist that offensive material be omitted, a script be shortened,
or even that a scene be reshot from a different, less sexualising
angle. The PCA fought liberal politics, suggestive sexuality,
indecent language, and any scandal of homosexuality. As we
shall see, the film version of *Cat* (1958) differed significantly
from Williams's script. Williams's 'play explores the discontent
of desire – and its polymorphous perversity as well. No
previous production, however, had dealt at such length and in
such depth with sexual questions' (Palmer and Bray, 8). The
Cat film was, however, heavily censored. Together with the
PCA, the Legion of Decency, the rating board of the Roman
Catholic Church, censored films by classifying them as 'A'
(Acceptable), 'B' (objectionable in parts), or 'C' (objectionable).
Receiving a rating of 'C' crippled a film's chances of making
money because theatres would not dare to show it or, if they
did, audiences, guided by the Legion's assessment, would be
likely to stay away.

Seen as a latent or repressed homosexual, Brick was far
removed from the strong male leads that dominated the
popular films of the decade, such as Charlton Heston's Moses
in *The Ten Commandments* (1955), the quintessential Cold War
film of the decade, or Gregory Peck's Captain Ahab in *Moby
Dick* (1956). Strong, hypermasculine images – such as John
Wayne, the warrior cowboy – were the norm because they

espoused family values, the hallowed foundation of democracy. Because of its homosexuality, alcoholism, adultery, Skipper's impotence, and Maggie's sexual aggressiveness, *Cat* hardly fostered the wholesome virtues espoused by the PCA and the Legion of Decency. The Pollitts were not the models of the happy 1950s American family that the PCA and the Legion wanted to see portrayed on screen. Thus, Williams's play, but not Brooks's 1958 screenplay, fomented a 'rebellion against social order' (Palmer and Bray, 163), challenging the creed of the conservative 1950s. For instance, by casting Brick as an ex-football player and a hunter, Williams shattered the stereotype that all gay men were effeminate.

Versions of *Cat on a Hot Tin Roof*

Like many of Williams's plays, the source for *Cat on a Hot Tin Roof* is one of his short stories, 'Three Players of a Summer Game' (1952), including the trio of Brick, Margaret, and Mary Louise Grey, the young widow of a doctor. In the story Margaret vanishes early and does not appear until the end; there is no Skipper or Big Daddy; and Brick's problem is ambiguous. The croquet game alluded to in Act One of *Cat* (7) is not fully developed in the story. In 1953, Williams also worked on the draft of a play, *A Place of Stone*, which became the intermediary script between 'Three Players' and *Cat*. In 1954, he showed a draft of *Cat* to the director Elia Kazan who insisted on three major changes: (1) have Big Daddy return in Act Three because he was 'too vivid and important a character to disappear from the play except as an offstage cry after the second act'; (2) make Maggie more sympathetic to audiences; and (3), show Brick experiencing a transformation as a result of his confrontation with Big Daddy and thereby reconciling with Maggie to end his 'moral paralysis'.

To ensure that the highly influential Kazan would direct *Cat* and to make his play commercially profitable, Williams agreed to the revisions but feared he would become 'a sort of ventriloquist's dummy for ideas which are not his own' ('Author and Director', 118). But when *Cat* was published in

1955, he included the two endings – his original one and the revised, Broadway version. Endlessly revising his plays, even after they were performed and printed, Williams created a new hybrid third act for the American Shakespeare production in 1974, incorporating some of Kazan's changes (e.g., Big Daddy returns in the third act and Maggie is more sympathetic) as well as others in his original draft, but the Brick–Maggie relationship still remained problematic. Williams's final version of *Cat* (1975) is used in this volume.

There has been a continuing debate about which version of *Cat* a director should choose to stage, although the Broadway version, which bears Kazan's heavy emendations, is usually not favoured. Even so, Kazan's decision to bring Big Daddy back on stage in Act Three has major implications for how the play is structured and staged.

Structure

Cat on a Hot Tin Roof, one of Tennessee Williams's most tightly crafted plays, runs about three hours. Divided into three acts, it has no scenes but includes two intermissions. Act Two, the turning point of the play, is rightfully the longest part and is flanked by two shorter acts, each approximately the same length. *Cat* is structurally a well-made play with a rising opening, complete with exposition giving us background information in Act One about Brick, Maggie, Big Daddy, etc., a turning point at the end of Act Two, and a climax in Act Three. Even though it follows the model of a well-made and seemingly realistic drama, Tennessee Williams still introduces non-realistic elements into the script, such as his highly expressionistic stage directions at the start of the play, those dealing with lighting, colour, and atmosphere.

Like a Greek tragedy, *Cat* follows the classical unities of action, time, and place. All events happen on a 'late and fair summer afternoon' and into that evening. The action revolves around Brick's relationships – with Maggie, Big Daddy, the Pollitt family, his friend Skipper, and himself. Big Daddy's health, fortune, and past sexual experiences also form a major part of the dramatic action. In fact, the fates of Big Daddy and Brick unfold like a classical tragedy adopted for modern times, with Southern landscapes, allusions, and dialects. Reflecting the play's continuous action, '*There is no lapse of time*' between Acts Two and Three. All the action in *Cat* also occurs in one place – in Brick and Maggie's bedroom – with a door to the adjoining bathroom and others leading to the gallery outside. For Brick, the bedroom is his sanctuary; for Maggie, it's her prison. For the other characters, it becomes the place where Big Daddy's sixty-fifth birthday party is celebrated or lamented. Symbolising barriers to communication, a constant flow of interruptions disrupt conversations in Brick's bedroom (Kolin, 'Obstacles'). Even with these interruptions *Cat* moves seamlessly, straightforwardly from one act to another.

Structurally, and poetically, *Cat* might also be compared to a musical composition. In many ways, the play is operatic, a score written for many different voices. Maggie's '*voice has range and music*' (9), and at times she sounds like a '*priest delivering a liturgical chant*' (40); offstage, Big Daddy's '*long drawn cry of agony and rage fills the house*' at the end of Act Three; birthday and children's songs, black work songs, music from a hi-fi, scat music, Wagner, and Beethoven also play during *Cat*. In his 'Notes for the Designer', Williams himself characterised the stage for *Cat* in musical terms: he wanted it to be roomy enough for a 'ballet'. Commenting on the 'musical structure' of the play, Brian Palmer claimed that Act One, where Maggie dominates, 'is practically an aria. Act Two focuses on a duet between Brick and Big Daddy; and Act Three is finally an ensemble' ('Swinging a Cat', 177).

Language

Cat on a Hot Tin Roof is poetic, compelling, explosive. Reviewing the 1955 premiere, Richard Watts characterised Williams's language as 'insistently vulgar, neurotic and ugly [yet it] still maintains a quality of exotic lyricism'. The blend of the lyrical and the ugly (cruel, lustful, distorted) nicely defines Williams's Southern grotesque. When *Cat* debuted on Broadway in 1955 Williams had to use such quaint words as 'rutten' (Mae and Gooper act like 'a couple of rutten peekhole spies' [55]), 'duckin', and 'frig' (as in Brick's imperative 'frig all dirty lies and liars!' [81]) in place of the four-letter taboo word and its participial variants. Soon after *Cat* opened, a New York City licence commissioner demanded that Big Daddy's elephant joke and other offensive language be cut. As Donald Spoto observed, 'the salty language, an off-color joke, and the psycho-sexual turmoil sent shock waves through audiences' (*Kindness*, 200). When Williams revised *Cat* in 1974–5, he updated and increased the profanities. Even today, productions of *Cat* have been labelled 'shocking' because of explicit language, and thus are often rated 'R' or 'restricted' (individuals of seventeen and younger are not admitted unless accompanied by an adult). In the 2008 *Cat*, James Earl Jones's Big Daddy shocked audiences 'with [his] unrestrained ribaldry' (Robertson).

Beyond doubt, Big Daddy's speech is expletive driven. It is poetic and filthy, sometimes simultaneously. In his *Memoirs*, Williams glowed: 'Big Daddy has a kind of crude eloquence of expression . . . that I have managed to give to no other character of my creation' (168). His speeches are peppered with four-letter words ranging from the mild 'damn', 'hell', and his favourite 'crap' to taboo words and blasphemies against the Deity. Listening to his colourful assortment of curse words, Big Mama admonishes him not to 'talk that way', but he bellows: 'I'll talk like I want . . . and anybody here that don't like it knows what they can do' (50). Big Daddy's speeches pulsate with obsessive repetitions that 'imitate the very mood and rhythms of . . . sexual intercourse', according to Dan Isaac (273) – 'All that stuff is bull, bull, bull!' (62) or 'I was Ochello's partner and the place got bigger and bigger and bigger and bigger' (51). Relishing sexual metaphors, Daddy Pollitt asks if Brick's injury in the middle of the night was the result of 'jumping or humping' in search of 'a piece o' poon-tang' (49); speaking of his own sex life with Big Mama, he brags that he 'laid her, regular as a piston' (72). But now dreading sex with her, he vows to find a 'choice one', 'strip her', and 'hump her from hell to breakfast'. Like his father, Brick digs into the lexicon of vulgarity. In denying homoerotic feelings on his part, Brick damns all 'fairies' and 'fuckin' sissies . . . [and] Queers' (79).

Given *Cat*'s intense sexuality, the human body is a frequent topic of conversation as well as a powerful visual symbol. Though 'crippled', Brick has lost none of his good looks. 'I actually believe you've gotten better looking since you've gone on the bottle' (16), claims Maggie. Muscular, tanned, and youthful, Paul Newman's body in the 1958 film was foregrounded with close-up shots of his chest. Less age-proof, Maggie retains her looks but declares, 'My face looks strained, sometimes, but [. . .] men admire it [her figure]. . . and last week . . . everywhere that I went men's eyes burned holes in my clothes' (30). James Earl Jones's Big Daddy was guilty of 'ogling Maggie from eyebrows to toenails' (Teachout). Exuding sexuality, Lindsay Duncan's Maggie (London, 1988) had 'carnivorous lips' and a 'debutante's sway' (Ratcliffe, 140). But beneath these external references to Brick's and Maggie's bodies lie sexual anxieties/confusions. Unable to discuss homosexual desire, a taboo subject, directly on stage in 1955 America, Williams projected the psychological torments and transformations gays experienced by showing their bodies re-aligned, torn apart, reconfigured, or deconstructed in a homophobic America.

According to David Savran, Williams used the language of fragmentation and marginalisation to 'characterise the inhabitants of the [homosexual] closet'. From his gay perspective he 'configure[ed] the female body constantly in danger of disintegrating' and in the process, 'throughout Act One Williams's stage directions teem with Maggie's body parts, arms, hands, throat'. By doing this, Savran contends, Williams was able to dramatise the homoerotic. Disengaged from a heterosexual, binary anatomy, 'the absent phallus [Skipper] becomes reinscribed in Maggie's body and allows her to be produced as the object of [male] desire'. As a result, Brick turns into 'the castrated male and Maggie the phallic woman'.

Animal imagery, another of Williams's staples, further helps to explain his characters. If the cat is Maggie's totem animal, capturing her wily tenacity, her nervous energy, and her fears, the elephant is Big Daddy's emblem of virility. More commonly, though, animal images evoke the cruelty or foolishness that transform human beings into grotesque creatures. Mae is cast as the 'monster of fertility' (10–11), and her five children as 'no-neck monsters' (7), who bear names (Dixie, Trixie, Buster, Sonny, Polly) that 'sound like four dogs and a parrot' (22). Big Daddy castigates the lot as 'little monkies'. Because of their beast-like behaviour, Gooper's brood descends down the great chain of being. His own name suggests a deformed creature with bulging body parts. Like a snake, Mae is heard 'hissing' at Maggie (114). Big Mama is comically likened to a charging rhino, 'an old bulldog' (25), or a pig when she grunts. In her patterned chiffon, she has 'the markings of some massive animal' (43). When the Pollitt clan gathers, 'the room sounds like a great aviary' (42). Big Daddy 'grins . . . wolfishly' about his future sex life.

Characteristic of Williams's plays, sickness symbolises greed, mendacity, and/or betrayals. Though the least mendacious character in *Cat*, Big Daddy nonetheless has an unquenchable desire for power and land. His inoperable intestinal cancer may possibly symbolise his aggressiveness and his own past homosexual relationships. A sick patriarch, a sick Big Daddy, suggests the entire family is ill. His sickness is both literal and symbolic: 'it's spread all through him and it's attacked all his vital organs, including the kidneys and right now he is sinking into uremia . . . poisoning of the whole system due to the failure of the body to eliminate its poisons', says Gooper (104). Brick is 'crippled' because of a jumping accident, but his physical malady suggests a deeper psychological and spiritual malaise – he is sick from guilt and cover-ups. (Maggie opens 'the sore of his friendship with Skipper'.) But his broken ankle is only the current manifestation of a lingering illness. As Big Mama recounts, Skipper's sickness affected Brick's crippling:

> That boy is just broken up over Skipper's death. You know how poor Skipper died. They gave him a big, big dose of that sodium amytal stuff . . . give him another big, big dose of it at the hospital and that and all of the alcohol in his system . . . just proved too much for his heart . . . I'm

scared of needles! I'm more scared of a needle than the
knife . . . I think more people have been needled out of
this world than – (93).

Considering Big Mama's fear of injections (and Williams's, as
in *Memoirs*, 232), it is frightening to think that 'Mae took a
course in nursing during the war' (99). Everyone in *Cat* is in
danger of being injected – Big Daddy will need a hypo and
Maggie acts like a '*child about to be stabbed with a vaccination
needle*' after dealing with Big Mama (29). Big Mama herself is
in danger of having a stroke because of her excitability. When
the family breaks the news to her about Big Daddy's cancer,
she thinks they are looking at her 'as if big drops of blood had
broken out on m'face' (95); her high blood pressure is 'riskin'
a stroke' (70). Later, Big Daddy warns her 'you better watch
that, Big Mama. A stroke is a bad way to go' (111). The
fireworks display in honour of Big Daddy's fatal birthday
party makes her 'feel a little bit sick at my stomach' (89),
possibly her sympathy pains for Big Daddy's gastro-intestinal
ravages. Given his alcoholism, Brick might be heading for
similar medical problems. Countering all these dire medical
reports, Maggie claims she is pregnant after consulting 'one of
the best gynecologists in the South' (113).

Fire imagery also spreads through *Cat*. Helping to visualise
the dangers that engulf the characters, Maggie describes Brick's
desire for Skipper and its devastating effect on their marriage
as a house fire: 'When something is festering in your memory
or your imagination . . . it's just like shutting a door and locking
it on a house on fire in hope of forgetting that the house is
burning. But not facing a fire doesn't put it out' (18). Brick
mockingly copies his wife's fire imagery: 'Lately, your voice
always sounds like you'd been running upstairs to warn
somebody that the house was on fire' (23). Big Daddy similarly
characterises Big Mama's European passions as 'just a big fire
sale, the whole fuckin' thing' (57–8). Ironically, his own house,
crammed full of Big Mama's European purchases, is ripe for a
fire sale. Bursts of fireworks, an omen of Big Daddy's last
birthday, suggest that the Pollitts are being consumed by the
flames of mendacity and hate. Yet fire both punishes and cleans

a house. The fireworks tolling Big Daddy's death might be interpreted as a birth announcement, thanks to Maggie's 'lie'.

Through its imagery, *Cat* shows how characters are trapped claustrophobically because of guilt, hate, and estrangement. Big Daddy and Brick, for example, 'talk, in circles' (68) and behind 'closed doors' (55). Without love, Brick and Maggie are 'caught in the same cage'. Ironically, Big Daddy's infamous final joke is about elephants in 'adjoinin' cages' (109). Maggie tells Brick that 'death was the only icebox' that could hold his epic love for Skipper, and Big Daddy warns his son that he'll hear 'a lot ... of unbroken quiet . . . in the grave' (60). Brick sees himself as trapped, having to sit 'in a glass box watching games' he could not play (76). Entrapment becomes cosmic alienation as well. Thinking he is cancer-free, Big Daddy claims he has 'come back' from 'the other side of the moon, death's country' (80). That's the place where light is shut out, and darkness is sealed in. Unfortunately, Mae cannot escape this dark prison either; she stands 'on the wrong side of the moon' (55), according to Big Daddy.

Characters

Creating memorable characters was Williams's trademark. 'My characters make my plays' ('Critic Says', 77), he declared. In *Cat* he used psychological realism to develop characters who act out of strong emotions and deep conflicts. Williams wanted his characters to tell their life stories; in fact, *Cat* is made up of the characters' confessional monologues. But Brick, Maggie, and Big Daddy also reveal various sides of Williams's own personality, his inner life. He seems torn between the melancholy Brick and the sexually frustrated Maggie.

Brick

Charles May rightly identifies Brick as 'the ambiguous center for all the characters' because he functions as 'the catalyst for the dramatic action'. We often see things from Brick's perspective. He is a central player in the confrontations with

Maggie in Act One and with Big Daddy in Act Two. Much of
Cat explores Brick's demons and how he battles with them.
Cool, depressed, and detached – adjectives that describe him
and how he communicates (or fails to do so). Leading a
dissipated life, Brick is a drunk who refuses to go to bed with
his wife and denies complicity in Skipper's death. He fights
being vulnerable, but his behaviour says otherwise. 'Give me
my crutch,' he orders Maggie. The crutch is Brick's signifier.
Frequently losing his balance and crawling along the floor,
Brick is a broken man – emotionally, physically, sexually, and
spiritually. He uses his crutch as an escape, a weapon, and an
emblem of his sexual/psychic wounds. It speaks for him when
he strikes out at Maggie.

Like Blanche in *Streetcar* and Tom in *The Glass Menagerie*,
Brick mirrors Williams's own sexual/psychic struggles. He
suffers from the same 'blue devils', fits of depression, that
plagued Williams. Moreover, as Margaret Bradham Thornton
observes, 'Williams was a part of a private world of gay men
who lived an existence secret from their families. In [*Cat*] he
creates men who have had unusually close relationships with
other men, who marry, and then have conflicts over the two
relationships' (9). Just like Williams's friends, Brick is the
estranged husband who protects his sexual identity in a
repressive society that would condemn him if he dared to
reveal his secret. Brick thus fulfilled a key role for Williams as
his creator. He allowed Williams to express his gay subjectivity
without 'coming out' as a gay playwright', according to Dean
Shackleford (106–7). Following the 1974 revival, Clive Barnes
thought that *Cat* was Williams's 'most honest play'. Williams
admitted it was his favourite. In order to write any play,
Williams claimed he had to fall in love with one of the
characters. In *Cat*, Brick is the object of masculine beauty for
Williams; 'a gay playwright [thus] places himself and his own
gaze at the center' of *Cat*, according to Shackleford. In the 1988
London *Cat*, Ian Charleson's Brick had 'the sort of charismatic
male divinity Williams must have had in mind when writing
the part' (Edwards, 136). Furthermore, as George Crandell
maintains, Brick becomes the spokesperson for Williams the
artist, crying out for attention and connection (438).

Brick plays other key roles. He is the prodigal son (eight years younger than Gooper) who throws his father's inheritance away. Once a conquering hero, Brick is the fallen, failed athlete reduced to announcing games rather than starring in them, and he forsakes even this job. (Ironically, he may be named after Jack 'Bud' Pollitt, a football star and acquaintance of Williams at the University of Missouri in 1931–2 [Hale].) An alcoholic, he chases the click that will bring him into oblivion. The large console on stage contains his liquor, TV, radio, and a hi-fi, all the 'comforts and illusions' (Williams, 'Notes for the Designer', 6) protecting him from self and the truth. The 1958 film of *Cat* included so much drinking that it is listed in the top 100 booziest movies ever made. Once a charming, confident lover, Brick is now a used-up stud gone dry. As we saw, Mae and Gooper label him a sexual deviate. Several classical myths further illuminate Brick's role. Achilles' legendary friendship with Patroclus may be a prototype for his affection for Skipper (Hurd); and Brick is certainly a broken Apollo (Thompson, 70). Drinking '*Echo Spring*' (Southern Bourbon) associates him with another classical figure, Narcissus, the beautiful young man who, seeing his reflection in a pool, jumped in and drowned. As Crandell argues, Brick's behaviour is 'fairly typical of the Narcissistic personality' (434) – self-love, rage, lack of empathy for others, need for constant attention. More favourably, Brick has been seen as the Sartrean existential hero trying to determine his own identity (Bak). But his sense of truthfulness is, at best, highly controversial.

Unquestionably, Brick is one of Williams's most complex and conflicted characters who raises key questions about mendacity – with others and with himself, including: (a) Is he gay? (b) What was his relationship with Skipper?

(a) *Cat* is problematic about Brick's sexual identity. Williams's own views on the subject are ambiguous, even contradictory. In the most famous stage direction in the play, Williams confessed, '*The bird that I hope to catch in the net of this play is not the solution of one man's psychological problem . . .* [but the] *interplay of live human beings in the thundercloud of a common crisis. Some mystery should be left in the revelation of character in a play'* (77). Rebutting the *New York Herald Tribune* critic Walter Kerr who attacked him for writing about a homosexual, Williams declared: 'Frankly, I don't want people to leave the Morosco Theatre knowing everything about all the characters they witnessed that night in violent interplay' ('Critic Says', 78). Three years after *Cat* opened, Williams again waffled in an interview with Arthur Walters: 'Brick is definitely not a homosexual. Brick's self pity and recourse to the bottle are not the result of a guilty conscience in that regard . . . He feels that the collapse and premature death of . . . Skipper . . . have been caused by unjust attacks against his moral character made by outsiders, including Maggie . . . It is his bitterness at Skipper's tragedy that has caused Brick to turn against his wife . . . although I do suggest that . . . there might have been unrealized abnormal tendencies' (Walters, 73).

The 'mystery' of Brick's sexual identity is at the heart of *Cat.* On the one hand, he never admits physical desire for Skipper and demonises homosexuals. Yet he describes intimate moments he shared with Skipper. Brick might not know or understand what homosexuality really is, dissociating his homosocial relationship with Skipper from a homosexual one. Or perhaps, though, he might be lying to himself. In that case, Brick's homophobia might be the mendacious façade for his true feelings about Skipper; he might be experiencing 'homosexual panic', the fear that he does in fact desire Skipper. This panic unsettles his self-image as the strong, heterosexual athlete hero (Arrell, 60–72). He is furious at Maggie for even suggesting to Skipper that he was gay. Or, more damningly, he might 'fail ethically because, finally, he seems willing to deny his nature and a lover before forfeiting his comfortable position in the world' (Paller, 112).

Each of these interpretations speaks to Williams's precarious position of couching Brick's sexual problems as 'mysteries'. In a 'Note of Explanation' (1955), he declared, 'I don't believe that a conversation, however revelatory, ever effects so immediate a change in heart or even conduct of a person in Brick's state of spiritual disrepair.' As we saw, Williams could not offend conservative Broadway audiences who supported his work. But by presenting Brick as 'conflicted',

Williams was able to keep his character's sexual identity a
mystery, leaving audiences wondering, asking probing
questions. The problematic ending that has disturbed so many
critics, therefore, may be Williams's way of drawing audiences
into Brick's moral paralysis, the world of his mendacity and
that of others. Ultimately, though, directors and actors have
great leeway in how they represent Brick.

(b) There seems to be little doubt that Skipper was gay and
that he desired Brick's love. But Brick, like Blanche DuBois in
Streetcar, rejects a homosexual who then commits suicide. This
surely is a sign of Brick's deliberate cruelty, the worst sin for
Williams. Moreover, Brick does not accept his responsibility
for Skipper's death. It leaves him depressed and brings into
question his maturity, his narcissism. By idealising Skipper's
friendship, Brick lessens every other relationship, for example
his marriage to Maggie and his obligations to Big Daddy. He
refuses to enter the adult world with its responsibilities to father
children and to run his father's estate. Instead, he prefers to
'foster the illusion that [he and Skipper] are still boys' (Winchell,
704). In such a world, Brick can be as close to Skipper as he
wishes. Their friendship is 'purged from any allusion to
homosexuality' since they live in a world of 'prolonged
adolescence' where 'homosocial discourse and activities are
acceptable and free from any stain of sexual transgression'
(Winchell, 705). In sum, Brick does not want to grow up; he
still wants to run the football field with his best friend to the
cheers of a fawning crowd – to be 'teammates forever' (38).

Maggie
Williams named the play in her honour. 'I am Maggie the
Cat,' she declares. In a letter to Lady Maria St Just, who
inspired the role of Maggie (*Five O'Clock Angel*, 167) and to
whom the play is dedicated, Williams insisted that Maggie was
the central character. 'The story [in *Cat*] must be and
remained the story of a strong determined creature (Life!
Maggie!) taking hold and gaining supremacy over and
converting to her own purposes a broken, irresolute man' (*Five
O'Clock Angel*, 110). Her final lines sum up her determination –

'Oh, you weak people, you weak, beautiful people! who give
up with such grace. What you want is someone to – take hold
of you. – Gently, gently with love hand your life back to you,
like somethin' gold you let go of' (115). Dominating the stage
in Act One, essentially a monologue lasting about an hour,
Maggie battles fiercely throughout *Cat*, and is responsible for
its startling revelation in Act Three.

She seems far removed from Williams's doomed Southern
belles – Amanda, Blanche, or Alma. Instead, Maggie prowls
with his more feisty heroines such as Serafina in *The Rose
Tattoo*, the Princess in *Sweet Bird of Youth*, or even Myrtle in
Kingdom of Earth. Like her namesake, Maggie is sleek, agile,
tenacious, clever, and seductive; she can manoeuver in tight
places and claw her way to the top. She is both a sex-starved
kitten and an alley fighter. She has the predatory instincts of
an animal yet she is also the spirit of life and love in *Cat*. Even
so, like many of Williams's women, Maggie fears losing her
dreams. In *Cat* they include: (1) regaining Brick's love; (2)
satisfying her sexual needs; and (3) receiving Big Daddy's
inheritance by having a child with Brick. As Maggie strives to
achieve these goals, we witness a woman who is lyrical, sexy,
determined, and inherently decent.

Like Brick and Big Daddy, Maggie takes on several roles.
Above all, she is a fighter/redeemer, resolved to overcome
a husband's rejection, a family's scorn, and a life of poverty.
While Brick is comfortable with 'the charm of the defeated',
she is not. Nothing stands in her path. At one point, she grabs
Brick's leg, allowing him to drag her across the stage,
demonstrating that she will never let go of him, never stop
loving him. She wants to save him from alcoholism; from his
greedy sibling; and from consuming guilt over Skipper's death.
She courageously tries to 'restore Brick's self-respect and faith
in his manhood' (Adler, 19). Like Brick, she is surrounded by
myths. She wins a 'Diana' trophy for archery (21) – a sign of
her skill at identifying and attacking a target. In Greek legend,
Diana was the huntress and protector of the woods. Evoking
the classical goddess, Maggie sees herself as Brick's hunting
partner and the protector of her husband's share in the Pollitt
plantation. Combining her feline and mythic roles, Maggie is

'endowed with the animal sinuosity and instinctive tenacity of a cat [and] the athletic aggressiveness of the Roman Diana' (Thompson, 68), but, ironically, she is also linked to Artemis, the Greek counterpart of Diana, famous for chastity. Nevertheless, Maggie is determined to end the enforced chastity imposed on her by Brick.

As Williams emphasised, Maggie is the life-force in *Cat*. 'I am alive,' she declares. She is a sexual dynamo, crying out for satisfaction. The empty bed, the centrepiece of the play, is her symbol of loneliness, sexual unfulfilment. She wants to reclaim it, make it her territory. A Southern Aphrodite, Maggie uses her beauty and charm to save her husband and dissuade Big Daddy from leaving the estate to Gooper. Portraying a woman in heat in 1955 was a daring move on Williams's part. Maggie's 'slip of ivory satin and lace' (7), her garter belt, her bracelets, her make-up rituals before the mirror, and her smoking, are signifiers of her sexual being. Her sexual identity points to how successful she could be as wife and mother. Moreover, she claims to bring 'life to this place that death has come in to' (115) by declaring she is going to produce a Pollitt heir. Maggie is thereby associated with renewal and redemption. A birth was associated with good fortune in the American South.

But only by dislodging Skipper's ghost from a place of prominence in Brick's heart and psyche can she give her husband a new identity/life. *Cat* is a play of triads, and the most significant is that of Brick, Maggie, and Skipper. Yet Maggie is a one-man woman. Brick's relationship with Skipper ostracises her as wife and woman; he has usurped her role as Brick's partner, turning her into the Other. When she and Brick 'double-dated at college' (37), she tells him 'it was more like a date between you and Skipper. Gladys and I were just sort of tagging along as if it was necessary to chaperone you!' (37). She uses her sex to counter Skipper's claims to Brick and so she can get her husband back to bed. Clearly, Maggie wanted to prove that Skipper was a homosexual to protect her marriage – 'Leave my husband alone.' But her breaking up Skipper's relationship with Brick has often elicited hostile responses. Robert F. Gross, for instance, insists that

Maggie 'gives male bonding a guilty conscience' (21). Seeing her victory really as a defeat, Mark Winchell claims Williams is 'using a symbolic code to tell others in the audience that Brick is vicariously making love to Skipper when he "humps" Maggie in Straw and Ochello's bed' (712). Similarly, queer readings of the play by David Savran and Dean Shackleford conclude that Maggie's body becomes the site where Brick and Skipper can finally meet, thus restoring Skipper's place as Brick's partner. Ironically, in trying to make love to Skipper, Maggie allowed herself and Brick's best friend 'to dream it was you, both of us!' (35).

Undeniably, the most problematic issue in *Cat* is whether Maggie will be successful in getting Brick back to bed. Kazan pushed for such an ending to demonstrate that Maggie 'was sympathetic, but she was strong. This revision resulted from exactly the kind of dialectic process that had occurred in all of Williams's work with Kazan' (Murphy, 101). Like Kazan, it was the way Hollywood wanted Williams's play to end in the 1958 film version. Resisting Kazan, Williams did not believe that Brick could undergo a complete transformation, which included an eager return to the marriage bed. Though Williams wrote a problematic, ambiguous conclusion, he nonetheless saw (and wanted) Maggie 'gaining supremacy'. Williams maintained that Brick 'will go back to Maggie for the sheer animal comfort of sexual release' and become 'her dependent' ('Critic Says', 78). And, to the very end of *Cat*, Williams portrays an invincible Maggie. She tells Brick, 'I am stronger than you . . . I can love you more truly.' Preparing for her long-postponed sexual conquest, she orders: 'Don't touch that pillow,' and declares 'I know what to do.' In one of the most telling lines in the play, she insists, 'We're going to make the lie true' (115). 'Lie' is a loaded word in *Cat*, a play filled with dirty secrets, mendacity, scandals, misrepresentations, and false accusations/reports. Big Daddy himself attests to Maggie's redemptive fertility: 'Uh-huh, this girl has life in her body, that's no lie' (112). Yet by making a 'lie' (a child) into truth (reality), she hopes Brick will love her again, and that Skipper will be laid to rest in Brick's conscience. In the end, Maggie wants Brick to find the intimacy with her that he

never did with Skipper or Big Daddy. Clearing this major
hurdle, she will have 'convert[ed] a broken, irresolute man'.
   But all Brick does is '*smil*[e] *with charming sadness*' (115). Is
this the charm of the defeated that Maggie earlier attacked
(i.e., that Brick has resolutely refused to accept a new identity
as husband and father)? Williams's final stage direction,
however, might translate into Brick's surrender to his wife's
pleas. In response to Maggie's 'What do you say?' Brick
answers, 'I don't say anything. I guess there's nothing to say.'
What does Brick's 'nothing' signal – his capitulation and
Maggie's triumph or her defeat and his victory in their
concession to mutuality? Significantly, *Cat* ends with a
question mark – 'Wouldn't it be funny if that was true?' –
echoing Big Daddy's words about Big Mama's love (52), which
do prove unshakably true. But controversy has swirled around
any resolution – Brick's, Maggie's, Kazan's, or Williams's. For
over five decades, critics have complained that Williams leaves
us in a muddle. Some have assaulted him for being 'cowardly'
and compromising his integrity as an artist. Others have, as
we saw, supplied their version of a satisfactory closure,
applauding Maggie's confidence or recuperating Brick's ideal
lost teammate through a rebirth of Skipper in sex with
Maggie. Yet, as productions of *Cat* over many decades and
several continents have established, if anyone can make lies
on the Pollitt plantation come true, it is Maggie, the agile cat.

Big Daddy

'I'm the boss here now,' shouts Big Daddy thinking he has
been spared from cancer. Bigger than life, Big Daddy is an
epic figure, an icon of masculinity, vitality, and power.
Williams claimed he bestowed 'a kingly magnitude' on him
(*Memoirs*, 234), an image reinforced by Big Daddy in his
belvedere like a god overseeing his empire in Act Three.
The sheer strength of his will, even when he is in pain, drives
Cat. The award-winning Broadway playwright Neil Simon
exclaimed that '*Cat on a Hot Tin Roof* is a beautiful play, but it's
got size to it, and there is no one around who does that
anymore' (Bryer, 77). Big Daddy contributes immensely to the

breadth and depth of Williams's play. Dressed in a white linen suit, smoking a huge cigar, he looks like the boss, the patriarch, a figure of authority and power. Physically large, robust actors such as Burl Ives, Charles Durning, or James Earl Jones have captured Big Daddy's dominating presence. Summarising the image Big Daddy creates, Ellen Donkin and Susan Clement point out:

> He effortlessly commands attention no matter where he goes, automatically positioning everyone around him as adjunct. His judgments are so powerful that they will resonate in everyone's head long after he is offstage. His presence is synonymous with control and power in ways that are profoundly linked to the social structures of marginalization and erasure. (3)

Everything about him is large. Big Daddy's possessions are big; he owns 'twenty-eight thousand acres of the richest land this side of the valley Nile' (74); his net worth comes 'close on ten million in cash an' blue-chip stocks'. (In the 2008 production, with a black cast, that sum had been increased to 80 million.) He is a force of nature. 'All of my life I been like a doubled-up fist . . . Poundin', smashin', drivin'!' (62). When he learns that his condition is not fatal, he declares, 'I want you to know that I breathed a sigh of relief almost as powerful as the Vicksburg tornado' (68). His commanding presence led Eric Bentley, in his review of the *Cat* premiere, to proclaim that 'Big Daddy is Williams's best male character' (29). Fortunately, director Elia Kazan prevailed over Williams to bring Big Daddy back in Act Three. According to Brenda Murphy, 'The most striking pictorial and kinetic statement Kazan encoded with the performance [of *Cat*] involved Big Daddy. He brought Big Daddy down front to address the audience four times' (116).

There were several Big Daddies in Williams's life. He grew up with a father, Cornelius Coffin (CC) Williams, who matched Big Daddy in size and intimidation. In fact, Williams admitted that *Cat* was about his relationship with his own father. The victim of Cornelius's frequent and sharp criticism, Williams tried to escape his father's harrowing questions and

rages. Only later in his life did Williams turn towards his
father with a kinder eye, evidenced in his late short story, 'The
Man in the Overstuffed Chair'. Colby H. Kullman indentifies
other big daddies in Williams's life – especially Kazan, who
through his 'strong influence and constant expression of
restraint and correction . . . cast and directed many of
Williams's plays but also defined his characters, called for new
lines, and changed endings' (668). The prototype for Big
Daddy, though, was the father of one of Williams's close
friends, Jordan Massee Senior, whom Williams had met in 1941
on St Simon's Island, off the coast of Georgia. According to
Williams's biographer Lyle Leverich, Massee Senior was 'an
imposing southern gentleman whose granddaughter had
dubbed him "Big Daddy", [and] was a true raconteur and used
expressions such as 'nervous as a cat on a hot tin roof' . . .
He was also endowed with an inexhaustible supply of stories
about plantation life . . . Tom [Tennessee] was clearly in awe
of the huge elder Massee in his white linen suit' (417).

Big Daddy is deeply invested in the homo-/hetero-sexual
politics of the play. He confesses that in his earlier years
'I bummed, I bummed this country till I was – ' and that he
'Slept in hobo jungles and railroad Y's and flophouses in all
cities' (77). Big Daddy's 'bummed' carries overtones of
sodomy. YMCAs and flophouses were also often locations of
homosexual trysts. Because of his past sexual experience, Big
Daddy for David Savran is a 'carrier of homosexuality' from
Straw/Ochello to his son Brick. Yet Big Daddy's sexual
alliances come at a price for some critics who see his intestinal
cancer as a punishment for sodomy, linking him to Emiel
Kroger, the old homosexual who suffers from the same
malady in Williams's short story 'The Mysteries of the Joy
Rio' (written in 1941; published in 1954). Despite Big Daddy's
homoerotic past, he brims over with heterosexual hedonism.
A keen observer of women's bodies, he regrets wasting his
seed on Big Mama. 'They say you got just so many and each
one is numbered' (65). Sounding like an older Stanley
Kowalski, whose *life has been pleasure with women, the giving and
taking of it* (*Streetcar*, Scene One), Big Daddy exults, 'I'm going
to pick me a choice one . . . I'll strip her naked and smother

her in minks and choke her with diamonds! Ha ha!' His joke
about the elephant also advertises Big Daddy's libido; it is no
coincidence that that the creature has a large proboscis
(phallic signifier), and that the husband bests the pachyderm
in size and vigour.

As patriarch, Big Daddy presides over one of the most
dysfunctional families in American drama. Williams chose a
symbolic time to stage *Cat*, Big Daddy's sixty-fifth birthday
party. As in his other plays (*Glass Menagerie, Streetcar, Baby Doll*,
etc.), a celebratory event turns into a ruined occasion. Rivalry,
jealousy, greed, anger and backbiting eat up the mendacious
Pollitt family. Gooper and his social-climbing wife scheme to
gain control of the plantation even before Big Daddy dies.
There is no fraternal love between Brick and Gooper. Sisters-
in-law Mae and Maggie cat-fight throughout the play. Even
though Big Daddy has not made a will, he has made up his
mind. 'Who said I was "leaving the place" to Gooper or
anybody. This is my sixty-fifth birthday! I got fifteen years or
twenty years left in me! I'll outlive *you*! I'll bury you an' have
to pay for your coffin,' he shouts at Brick. He bluntly tells
him, 'But why in hell . . . should I subsidize a fool on the
bottle?' (74). Moreover, Big Daddy finds his grandchildren,
sired by Gooper and breeder-wife Mae, obnoxious, intrusive,
animal-like. He cannot even remember their names. Without
necks, the children are unnatural, unlovable, unconnected to
their patriarch. 'Their heads are directly connected to their
stomachs, symbolizing their greed/appetite for food, attention,
control' (Dukore, 97). Given Big Daddy's strong personality,
however, it is no wonder that the Pollitts inherited his
boisterous ways.

But they have not received his heart. That sensitive side of
Big Daddy is revealed only in conversations with his favoured
son Brick. Their confrontation is one of the most powerful
father/son scenes in modern American drama, alongside
those in Arthur Miller's *Death of a Salesman* and *All My Sons*,
and Eugene O'Neill's *Long Day's Journey into Night*. Uncovering
psychic wounds after years of 'talking in circles', Brick and
Big Daddy at last bare their souls. Determined to save his son
from self-destruction, Big Daddy declares, 'I am going to

straighten you out' and probes Brick's façade with dagger-like accuracy. Trying to rouse Brick out of guilt and spiritual lethargy, Big Daddy gives him no opportunity to evade or downplay his questions. He refuses to allow Brick to use Maggie as an excuse for the way his relationship ended with Skipper and accuses Brick of the mendacity that will ruin his life. He wants Brick to grow up and accept the responsibility for Skipper's death. 'This disgust with mendacity is disgust with yourself' (84). His confrontation with Brick is fast-paced, throbbing, and, at times, physical. He pushes him down and takes his crutch. But when Brick '*loses his balance* [and] . . . *grabs the bed and drags himself up*', Big Daddy offers him his hand, which at first Brick rejects, but then a domineering father becomes the tender loving parent, declaring, ' "Well I want yours. Git up!" *He draws him up, keeps an arm about him with concern and affection*' (80). Wanting to ease Brick's pain, physical and mental, Big Daddy welcomes the prodigal home to his arms.

Exploring how large issues such as love, life, and death are sewn into Big Daddy's character, *Cat* merits being seen as a tragedy of universal importance. Like a tragic protagonist, Big Daddy is proud, valiant; he is Williams's King Lear. Like Lear, he rages against his fate and the mortality it imposes on him. He battles death itself. His words to Brick, 'Life is important. There's nothing else to hold onto' (56), segue into the Dylan Thomas epigraph to *Cat*, 'father . . . Rage, rage against the dying of the light'. Ironically, the old man wants life, while his son Brick wants death (Dukore, 96). Big Daddy's imprecation, leaving his voice '*hoarse*' at the end of Act Two, can be likened to Lear's rage against injustice on the moor (Act III.1). In one of his most impassioned speeches, Big Daddy tragically comments on man's existential strength in the face of death:

> Ignorance – of mortality – is a comfort. A man don't have that comfort, he's the only living thing that conceives of death, that knows what it is. The others go without knowing which is the way that anything living should go, go without knowing, without any knowledge of it, and yet a pig squeals, but a man sometimes, he can keep a tight mouth about it. Sometimes he – (61)

Like King Lear, Big Daddy is surrounded by a family who betray him and by retainers (Reverend Tooker and Dr Baugh) who lie to him. Like Lear's eldest daughters, his rapacious children (Gooper, Mae, and their hoard) seek to rob him of his kingdom. As in *King Lear*, too, Williams included a raging storm in Act Three symbolising the larger cosmic forces that threaten Big Daddy's hold on the plantation, family, self, and life. But like Lear or Agamemnon, Big Daddy has a tragic flaw – his overweening pride, his defiant egotism. Believing he is cured, he struts across the stage thinking he is still boss. Speaking of Maggie and Mae, he declares: 'I got a surprise for those women. I'm not gonna let go for a long time yet if that's what *they're* waiting for' (53). But learning the truth about his medical condition, Big Daddy, like great tragic heroes, experiences the terror of a *peripetia*, a reversal of fortune. He leaves *Cat*, though, not as a defeated victim but as a force that death will have to reckon with.

Big Mama

Compared with her husband, Big Mama is a secondary character who seems easy to stereotype as clownish, a garrulous, hysterical woman, a coarse harridan. Yet she manifests a much more noble self and serves an important structural function in *Cat*. Like Maggie, she is married to a man who has rejected her, leaving her sexually starved. It has been four long years since Big Daddy has made love to her yet she remains loyal and caring. According to Nancy Tischler, Big Mama is a 'beautiful, strong study in unfilled love' (201). Even the thought of Big Daddy's having cancer evokes a painful gesture of love from her – '*Big Mama's chest heaves and she presses a fat fist to her mouth*' (50). Yet critics have seen her actions as a 'distorted manifestation' of Maggie's plight (Mayberry, 361). Obviously, she does not have Maggie's voice and spirit. In the hands of such veteran actresses as Judith Anderson, Kim Stanley, or Kate Reid, all of whom have tackled the role, Big Mama aspires to greater heights. Though she lacks her husband's overwhelming drive, she comes forward as his staunch supporter when, at the end of the play, she adopts his voice (including his swear words) to thwart Gooper and Mae's coup. She is a mix of laughter (often at her expense) and tears. Like so many women of her generation, she has sublimated her desires for the welfare of the family. Only a grandmother like Big Mama could think Gooper's brood was adorable. At the end of the play, when she asks if she can accompany Big Daddy to the belvedere and he allows her to, she reaches the apex of her life – to be valued as his caring wife.

Jack Straw, Peter Ochello, and Skipper

The ghosts of these gay men haunt *Cat on a Hot Tin Roof*. Though they never appear on stage, these characters embody many of the sexual anxieties in *Cat* and express Williams's own problematic attitudes toward homosexuality. Straw, Ochello, and Skipper join the company of other absent, dead, gay characters in Williams whose claims on their respective plays long survive the grave – Allen Grey in *Streetcar*, Sebastian Veneble in *Suddenly Last Summer*, or Williams's favourite poet, Hart Crane in *Steps Must be Gentle*. To accommodate a homophobic Broadway theatre, and perhaps to assuage his own psyche (Paller), Williams erased the presence of gay characters, although through them he was able to voice the cries of a gay man. In his early and late plays, Williams had no qualms about including overtly gay characters on stage. His first gay character, a transvestite, Queenie, was one of the prisoners in *Not About Nightingales* (1938) and, towards the end of his career, Williams openly portrayed his homosexuality through the writer and his own personification, August, in *Something Cloudy, Something Clear* (1981). But none of his plays feature as many gay figures, absent or present, as does *Cat*.

The play was guardedly subversive for its times. Williams describes the gay couple of Straw and Ochello as 'a pair of old bachelors who shared this room all their lives together' and whose relationship 'must have involved a tenderness which was uncommon' ('Notes for the Designer'). John Clum stresses that Williams did not stereotype the pair but presented them as shrewd and sensitive, running a 'successful enterprise' and

not 'self hating' like Skipper. Unlike his son's relationship with
Skipper, Big Daddy was empowered through his partnership
with Straw and Ochello. Keep in mind, though, that Williams's
admiration for the couple's *'uncommon tenderness'* was expressed
in an authorial stage direction, not in lines spoken before an
audience. According to Savran, Williams thus 'reveals his
homosexuality in extremely conflicted ways, as a focus of
desire and scandal'. For example, his 'naming of these two
characters . . . provide[d] significant insight into [Williams's]
oblique way of approaching the subject of homosexuality'
(Cañadas, 60). 'Straw' implies that as a homosexual 'he is a
man of straw, a man of no substance'; and Ochello 'suggests
the Italian word, *occhiello*, meaning "buttonhole" or "eyelet"'.
In using these names, Williams 'introduced metaphoric
allusions to male homosexuality [with] specific reference to
sexual penetration' (Cañadas, 58).

Skipper is *Cat*'s sexual barometer. Emerging like a dangerous,
guilty secret from Brick's past, he is at the centre of Brick's
sexual, marital, and filial conflicts. As Brick's team/roommate
at Ole Miss, Skipper evokes the glory days of their
championship football careers. Brick emphatically denies that
there was anything 'dirty' or 'sissie' about his friendship with
Skipper. 'Skipper and me had a clean, true thing between us!
– had a clean friendship . . . Oh, once in a while he put his
hand on my shoulder or I'd put mine on his, oh, maybe even,
when we were touring the country in pro-football an' shared
hotel-rooms we'd reach across the space between the two beds
and shake hands to say goodnight' (81). By characterising his
relationship as 'clean', 'the one', and 'pure', Brick, according
to Judith Thompson, is equating it with 'philosophical terms
of Platonic absolutes in Ideas of the Good, the Beautiful, the
true'. Yet when Maggie agrees with Brick that his relationship
with Skipper was ideal, as in Greek mythology, she ironically
alludes to its homosexual undercurrents, since classical myths
of male friendship were often rooted in homoerotic desire.

Like the names Williams uses for the 'old bachelors',
'Skipper' onomastically underscores the sexual tensions in *Cat*
and those harrowing Williams himself. Paller argues that the
name alludes to Kip Kiernan, the young Canadian dancer

with whom Williams fell in love in the summer of 1940 in
Provincetown, Massachusetts, but who broke his heart. Through
Skipper, Williams 'was venting anger, exercising a psychological
revenge on Kip Kiernan who died of a brain tumor'.
Skipper's name also suggests boyhood immaturity, a sign,
in terms of a 1955 psychotherapy, of latent homosexuality,
according to Clum. Like Skipper, Brick refuses to grow up, to
become a man, but, instead, is locked into a world of college
football. The name 'Skipper' also links the nautical and the
sexual, a crucial connection for Williams. Sailors were among
the primary agents through whom he sought to fulfil his
homoerotic desires and he often stereotypes them as sexualised
figures – for example, *Glass Menagerie*, *Streetcar*, *Rose Tattoo*,
Something Cloudy. Finally, the name 'Skipper' physicalises Brick's
condition. Hobbling along with his crutch, Brick becomes a
skipper, a halting, wounded and defeated man (Kolin, 215).

Gooper and Mae
Grasping, vicious, and jealous, Gooper and Mae are foils to
Brick and Maggie in Williams's dysfunctional family drama.
Gooper is a fawning, untrustworthy son who has the audacity
to tell Big Mama: 'I've always loved Big Daddy in my own
quiet way. I have never made a show of it, and I know that
Big Daddy has always been fond of me in a quiet way, too,
and he never made a show of it neither' (102). Big Daddy has
never been quiet about a thing, least of all his contempt for
his elder son. 'I hate Gooper and Mae an' know that they hate
me' (74). Gooper likes power, and he uses an assortment of
stratagems to win Big Daddy's plantation, including making
his children pawns, protecting Big Mama's interests, and
denouncing Maggie's 'lie'. The noisy games that his 'monsters'
play with their cap pistols comically parallel their father's
assaults against Big Daddy and Brick. Even the name of
Gooper's law partner – Tom Bullit – suggests the combative
tactics he employs to secure Big Daddy's fortune for himself
and his 'screamin' tribe' of monsters.

Gooper symbolises a character type Williams loathed – the
American corporate man of the 1950s, the arch-conservative

hypocrite. Big Daddy is the corporation Gooper wants to take over, but the old man is too shrewd to fool. When he sees the trusteeship papers scattered about Brick's room, knowing they really spell 'nothing', Gooper and Mae hurriedly gather them up, stage business that underscores their cover-ups and trickery. Behind everyone's back, Gooper has garnered a cache of damaging papers – power of attorney to 'cut off' Brick and Maggie's credit (10), a trusteeship for the estate, reports on Big Daddy's prognosis from Oschner's, and possibly a court order sentencing his younger brother to Rainbow Hill. As Maggie warns Brick, when news breaks about Big Daddy's fatal condition, 'Brother Man and his wife . . . hustl[ed] down here . . . And why so many allusions have been made to Rainbow Hill lately. You know what Rainbow Hill is? Place that's famous for treatin' alcoholics an' dope fiends in the movies!' (10). If Gooper gains control of Big Daddy's fortune, Brick is destined to be locked up.

Biographically, Gooper evokes the fraternal tension and rivalry between Williams and his younger brother Dakin. A football star, military hero, and successful lawyer, Dakin was Cornelius Williams's favourite, while Tennessee was attacked as the Other. Just as Gooper intended to send Brick to Rainbow Hill, Dakin was responsible for committing his brother to the psychiatric ward of Barnes Hospital in St Louis in 1969 for alcohol and drug abuse. Tennessee's greatest fear was being committed, as his sister Rose was in the 1930s for her schizophrenia. Dakin was also responsible for having his brother buried in the place Tennessee despised – St Louis (or 'St Pollution', as he called it). A further (but kindly) parallel between Dakin and Gooper surfaces in Gooper's shrewd handling of money, a talent that Tennessee later benefited from when he sought his brother's advice on finding tax shelters. Dakin referred to himself as Tennessee's 'professional brother'. What Tennessee Williams did, then, in *Cat* was to switch his younger brother's life with Brick's older brother's resulting in an overall unflattering portrait of Dakin Williams (Spoto, *Kindness*).

Mae also embodies a character type frequently satirised by Williams – the social-climbing club woman whose passion is backbiting. The gossiping women in *The Rose Tattoo*, *Spring Storm*, or *Orpheus Descending* are Mae's compatriots, as are the sarcastic matrons in Williams's other plays. The snooty socialites who visit flophouses in *Fugitive Kind* (1937) or nursing homes in *This is the Peaceable Kingdom* (1970) can also claim kinship with Mae. Unrelentingly repugnant, Mae is a fitting consort for her crafty husband. She is condescending to Big Mama, spiteful to Maggie and Brick, and stuffed with vanity. Yet Mae's looks belie her self-image. She is a 'monster of fertility'. In recent productions, she has been portrayed as a bottle-blonde loud-mouth. Appropriately, she comes from a family of crooks. Her 'ole Papa Flynn . . . barely escaped doing time in the Federal pen for shady manipulations on th' stock market' (13). Mae's father sounds like the swindlers arrested for their Ponzi schemes during the 2009 recession in America. Like her cheating father, Mae hopes to manipulate Big Daddy with her inflated stock of monsters. She is all those things that Maggie is not and vice versa.

Production History

Broadway
Cat premiered on Broadway at the Morosco Theatre on 24 March 1955 and ran until 17 November 1956, for a total of 694 performances. In a long line of Broadway premieres (*Glass Menagerie*, 1945; *Streetcar*, 1947; *Summer and Smoke*, 1948; *Rose Tattoo*, 1951; *Suddenly Last Summer*, 1958; *Sweet Bird of Youth* 1959; *Night of the Iguana*, 1961), *Cat* won Williams his second Pulitzer Prize and the New York Drama Critics' Circle Award. Directed by Elia Kazan, with stage designs by Jo Mielziner and costumes by Lucinda Ballard, *Cat* boasted the same artistic team that helped Williams receive his first Pulitzer for *Streetcar* in 1947. The actors in *Cat* received undiminished praise. Barbara Bel Geddes was applauded for her 'authoritative and appealing' Maggie (McClain) and for her uncapped energy. Ben Gazzara's anguished Brick was 'handsome, melancholy, sensitive' (Atkinson), and even though he had to 'hop, fall and drag himself' across the stage, he did so with 'great grace' (Hawkins). His depressed Brick set the tone for later actors

who took the role. Folk-singer Burl Ives, then forty-six years old and whose appearance in *Cat* was his first professional acting role, was hailed for his 'Rabelaisian' Big Daddy (Kerr), an 'unforgettable character' who questions an 'empty existence' (Coleman). Despite Big Daddy's charisma, many critics faulted his gratuitous and disturbing vulgarity. Kudos went to Mildred Dunnock (Linda Loman in *Death of a Salesman*) for her interpretation of Big Mama who 'has unexpected strength of character' (Atkinson) and was both 'fragile and touching' (Chapman). Pat Hingle's Gooper was suitably 'shifty' and shrewd, while Madeleine Sherwood as the venal and annoying Mae, oversaw 'the South's most horrifying children' (Hawkins).

Cat itself did not fare as well. While the critics handily recognised Williams's craftsmanship, his ability to offer shocking theatre, and his powerful dialogue, they found his new play 'tormented and tormenting' (Watts), a work that left audiences torn between 'frustration and revulsion' (McClain). Reviewers sensed that Kazan's changes were very much at odds with Williams's original script. Chapman complained that 'this time Williams has out-frustrated himself by failing to remain in control of his own play'. The critics also took Williams to task for *Cat*'s confusing characterisations, its unbelievable ending, and its revolting subject matter. Zeroing in on Brick's submerged homosexuality, Kerr complained that 'truth dodges around corners' and, consequently, judged *Cat* to be 'a flawed work', telling his readers: 'You will believe every word that is unspoken; and you may still long for some that seem not to be spoken.' He further warned that Williams's 'new play' lacks the 'staggering clarity of *Streetcar*'. Kerr's point of view was echoed over the next half century. Chapman, however, had no trouble speaking the unspeakable – Brick was a 'drunkard and a queer'. Overall, the problems the critics identified in the *Cat* premiere did not go away in the four major Broadway revivals the play has had up to 2009.

Over twenty years passed between the *Cat* premiere and its first Broadway revival. Initially performed at the American Shakespeare Festival in Stratford, Connecticut, in the summer of 1974, *Cat* opened at the ANTA Theatre on 24 September and closed on 8 February 1975 for a total of 160 performances.

It was the first time Williams's definitive third act was staged in the US, which incorporated Kazan's suggestion from the Broadway script to bring Big Daddy back in Act Three as well as changes Williams made in his original draft. In the process, Williams provided a 'more sensitive handling of the Brick and Maggie relationship' (Barnes), but the couple's reconciliation was still problematic. Snyder complained that in the new version of *Cat* 'there are no winners in this stark contest'. But the play had changed with the times. Homosexuality and women's sexual hunger were no longer as shocking as they were in 1955. Consequently, the emphasis fell on the family's deceit and hate – 'They all seem to have a cancer . . . eating away at their insides' (Probst).

If *Cat* itself still worried critics, this production nevertheless justified the high praise it earned. Deftly directed by Michael Kahn, it starred Elizabeth Ashley as Maggie; Keir Dullea as Brick; Fred Gwyne as Big Daddy; Kate Reid as Big Mama; Charles Siebert as Gooper and Joan Pape as Mae. Hands down, Ashley's Maggie was the star, a performance that received Williams's enthusiastic endorsement. Her Maggie was 'sensuous, wily, febrile, gallant, scorchingly Southern' (Kalem); she was the 'calculating bitch' as well as the 'ingenious' wife pleading for love (Wilson). Ashley's Maggie had displaced Brick as 'Williams's mouthpiece' (Sharp). On the other hand, Keir Dullea's Brick was disappointing. Playing a brooding Brick in the tradition of Gazzara and Newman, Dullea was no match for Ashley; he was underwhelmed. Injecting humour into Brick's role was a fresh interpretation, although Dullea's 'boyish laughter undercut' the play (Wilson). Gwyne's (Herman in the *Munsters*) Big Daddy was lanky, too young, and resembled Abraham Lincoln. Looking more like 'Tall Daddy' than Big Daddy, he lacked Burl Ives's 'roguish animal magnetism' (Kalem).

Thirty-five years after *Cat* premiered, the second Broadway revival made history, too. Howard Davies, who two years earlier had directed the play in London, brought *Cat* to the Eugene O'Neill Theatre in March 1990 using Williams's original script (1955), unedited by Kazan, for the first time on Broadway. The only changes Davies made were to keep the storm that Kazan inserted and to create a naturalistic set. Edwin Wilson glowingly wrote: 'This present version suggests Williams's first instincts about the play have been right after all.' William Henry agreed, claiming that there was now 'an altogether redemptive final scene'. Yet Jack Kroll insisted that the third act remained the 'weak limb' of the play.

There was nothing weak about their production; in fact Kathleen Turner and Charles Durning were credited for even mounting a second revival. With her 'throaty molasses voice' (Barnes), Turner's Maggie was the star of this *Cat*, a position Williams's original script intended. Flirtatious, determined, funny, and in love with her own sexuality, she 'prowls the stage in a second-skin slip, brushing her electric blond mane, tugging her nylons up her long legs, rigging her garter belt, applying mascara with spit and polish' (Kroll). Though Turner's cat was red hot, critics begged her to 'expose her emotions a shade more' (Wilson), especially in expressing her love for Brick. Durning's Big Daddy in his rumpled white suit, and vaudeville-sized cigar, was a 'hybrid of red-neck cut-up and aristocratic tragedian . . . a cracker barrel Lear and Falstaff in one' (Rich). Though he did not appear in Act Three, Durning's overwhelming presence as Big Daddy still dominated. Brick, played by Daniel Hugh Kelly, who paraded on stage in his bath towel, could have been more forceful, his anger more intense. Yet when he defended his relationship with Skipper, Kelly gave 'an impassioned hint of the noble figure who inspired worship from all who knew him' (Rich). According to Barnes, though, he never captured 'the complexity of a man who betrayed the thing he so loved and [also] possibly his own sexuality'. WABC TV's Joel Siegel bluntly announced: 'We realize he [Brick] is a homosexual even if he doesn't.' However brilliant the acting, this *Cat* also was dated for many critics: 'The 50s sexual tension now seems overripe; its hush-hush attitude toward cancer and scandal over childlessness seems almost quaint' (Winer, 358).

Like the second revival, the third revival of *Cat* came to Broadway, at the Music Box Theatre, on 3 November 2003, via London where the play had been directed by Anthony Page two years earlier, but with a different cast. Despite Page's superlative craft and an all-star cast, this revival was possibly the least successful of the four thus far. Under Page's direction, *Cat* manifested a tragic-comic spirit, mixing the hilarious with the mendacious, an apt combination for Williams's Southern grotesque. Yet Howard Kissel smarted from the 'sardonic, angry humor' in the play. Ned Beatty's Big Daddy was the driving force behind this *Cat* rather than Ashley Judd's Maggie. Despite having a smaller frame than Burt Ives or Charles Durning, Beatty was 'emotionally towering' (Murray); 'his prickly spirit catches all the cunning and cruelty of Big Daddy's vulgar energy' (Lahr). Ben Brantley exulted in Durning's performance, calling him a 'jig dancing bantam, a Napoleonic figure who has lulled himself into power'. Beatty's Big Daddy was likeable and feared at the same time. Though ravishingly beautiful, comic, and steely, Judd's Maggie 'showed little spontaneity' (Brantley); 'we don't see her suffocating under the threat of mendacity' (Murray). As Elyse Sommer put it, her Maggie 'was more fidgety and cool than fiercely hungry'. Maggie must show spite as well as sensitivity. Jason Patric's representation of Brick had a limited 'emotional range' – from amusement to annoyance (Murray). He 'compacts Brick into cement' for Lisa Schwarzbaum. In his confrontation with Beatty, Patric could not muster up the tension, hurt, and rage inside Brick. Even more disappointingly, he did not show 'the sexual ambiguity' that crippled Brick (Kissel). Assessing Judd and Patric's chemistry, Schwarzbaum bristled: 'She's unsure and he's unreceptive'. Surprisingly, Margo Martindale's Big Mama, a 'large woman whose charm bracelet jiggles along with the wattles under her chin', lifted the Pollitt matriarch above the bovine stereotype that has stamped the role (Lahr).

The fourth Broadway revival (6 March to 22 June 2008) was a landmark production. It was the first time a professional all-black cast staged *Cat* on Broadway and featured James Earl Jones (*Great White Hope*) as Big Daddy, Phylicia Rashad (TV's *Bill Cosby Show*) as Big Mama, Terrence Howard (*Hustle and Flow*) as Brick, and Anika Noni Rose (*Dreamgirls*) as Maggie. Though the director Debbie Allen 'wisely pushes past the issue of race' (Brantley), her *Cat* should be seen in terms of contemporary racial issues. During the spring and summer of 2008, Barack Obama electrified the world in his bid to be the first African American president. Change had come to the American theatre too, as Broadway attracted more black audiences than ever before, eager to see their favourite black stars on stage. In fact, seventy to eighty per cent of the audiences for Allen's black *Cat* were African Americans (Fisher). Critics asked if indeed Broadway had gone black. There was no question that Williams's 'tale of dirty politics among a filthy right, white family in the Mississippi Delta in 1955 [was] universal enough to withstand color-blind treatment' (Portantiere). While she strove not to change Williams's language, Allen omitted the elephant joke and shifted the time-frame closer to 1990 when Ole Miss was no longer segregated (as it was in 1955). But she was faulted for the changes she made in Williams's dramaturgy – that is, for having a saxophonist play a bluesy score before each act and for placing the major characters in a confessional spotlight which 'carr[ies] us out of the naturalistic world of the play' (Denton). Even more seriously, though, she was accused of sentimentalising Williams's script, taking *Cat* down to the level of black sit-com and lowering its 'emotional intensity, bringing it down to a simmer' (Dziemianowicz).

That charge could not be levelled at James Earl Jones's Big Daddy. With his resounding baritone voice and impressive stature, Jones's Big Daddy made history. As Clive Barnes proclaimed, his 'portrayal [of Big Daddy] with bluster and subtlety . . . will surely leave a permanent mark on a role he both inhabits and embodies.' Terry Teachout declared 'Jones gets Big Daddy – the pride, the contempt, the half-concealed terror.' 'I always wanted to play that cracker', Jones laughingly told ABC News (Fisher). His intensity contrasted with Terrence Howard's soft spoken and, even more inebriated and detached, Brick. In sum, Howard's performance received mixed reviews. Portantiere hailed his Brick as one of the 'most complex, fully realized . . . human portrayals' which escaped 'the two note trap of playing him as "taciturn and angry" throughout . . . he is often smiling and even laughing over the absurdities' on the Pollitt estate. But Martin Denton complained that Howard 'plays up the detachment to a point where he's almost not there sometimes'. For Brantley, Howard 'is wearing his character's pain all too palpably, mopping his eyes and tearfully bleating his lines . . . [turning] Brick into a wounded boy instead of the willfully numbed creature he must be to challenge Big Daddy.'

Rose's Maggie more than compensated for Howard's anaesthetised performance. Dressed in a slinky slip and falling backwards onto a sumptuous bed to adjust her garter belt, Rose exuded a steamy sexuality, yet she possessed an incredible shrewdness, anticipating how to act and react to Brick's and his family's attacks. Brantley affirmed that Rose's Maggie 'pretty much owns the show when she is on stage'. However, Rose may have paid a price for Maggie's intensity. Dziemianowicz found that she 'shows us Maggie's sexual claims but not the vulnerability that would snare us as allies'. Williams's script asks a great deal from any actor playing Maggie; she has to be sexual, shrewd and honest, yet also reveal a hurting, vulnerable side. Rashad's Big Mama undeniably showed her character's pain. For Clive Barnes, she was 'broken and defiant', but she also provided 'tragic-comic relief as the shrill, underappreciated Big Mama'. Arrindell Anderson's Mae was 'too smart, too well put together' and too good-looking (Denton).

British productions

Two and a half years after the US debut, *Cat* premiered in Britain on 30 January 1958. Produced and directed by Peter Hall, this *Cat* starred the American actress Kim Stanley as Maggie, Paul Masse as Brick, and Leo McKern, wearing shoulder pads, as Big Daddy. Williams's play (with his original third act intact) had to be staged as a club performance – at the Comedy Theatre in London – because the Lord Chamberlain banned it from public theatres for its objectionable subject matter. Brick's latent homosexuality, as well as the sexual excesses of the other characters, stirred up a controversy in the UK. The reviewer for the *News Chronicle* hailed *Cat* as 'Williams's most enthralling play', while the *Daily Mail* critic found it Williams's 'cruellest but at times most dramatic' work (quoted in 'London Sees'). An unsigned reviewer for the *Times*, however, attacked *Cat* not so much for its homosexuality as for the 'animal ferocity' of its characters – 'they cease to resemble human beings'. According to the reviewer, Williams wrongly 'injected . . . into his leading characters . . . a special serum of greed, sexual frustration, sexual longing, and sexual uncertainty' that was lethal. Unfortunately, Stanley's 'touchingly shameless' Maggie lacked the 'wiry defiance' the character needed and McKern's Big Daddy was 'not ideally suited' to the part, 'playing it a little outside of the character'. Masse's Brick existed in 'a kind of gentle haze'. Though Kenneth Tynan recognised that *Cat* was 'a magnificent play', he faulted Hall for his 'lethargic pace; he stresses everything except what needs stressing' (203), and thought Masse was 'callow and absurdly unprepared for a searching test like Brick', while Stanley was a 'gifted' Maggie, though she lacked the tension the role demanded.

When Howard Davies's production of *Cat* opened in London on 17 February 1988 on the National Theatre's Lyttelton stage, it made British theatre history for several reasons. It was the first production of Williams's play in the UK for thirty years and the first time *Cat* was staged at a public theatre there. Ironically, as Davies's *Cat* was playing, the House of Lords was debating the so-called 'notorious' Clause 28, banning the funding of any art project that promoted homosexuality. Davies used Williams's restored original third act which presented a less sympathetic Maggie. Nonetheless, Lindsay Duncan's Maggie successfully competed with Eric Porter's Big Daddy. It would appear that Williams's *Cat* had improved with age. The critics lavished praise on him for his 'masterpiece', which 'demonstrates that poetry in the theatre does not necessarily consist of heightened language and blank verse' (King). The actors spoke Williams's poetry with an accurate Southern accent, though at times it was hard to understand for London audiences. For the most part, the acting was judged superlative. Looking 'even Burlier than Ives', Portman did not simply replicate his American counterpart but brought a new perspective to the role of Big Daddy – subtlety and 'an intelligence and worldliness that begin to look wise' (Ratcliffe). His grey locks and beard, powerful voice, and compassion made Porter stand out. With her golden hair and smooth white shoulders, Duncan represented a Maggie that looked a little too Hollywood – 'somewhere between Marilyn Monroe and Elizabeth Taylor' (Radin). Still, she was a 'triumphant mixture of sexual hunger, venomous wit, and smouldering defiance, not least in the way she angles her head when she announces her pregnancy as if to defy her husband or anyone else to say her nay' (Billington). Succumbing to Maggie's power, Ian Charleson (star of *Chariots of Fire*) played a brooding, even catatonic at times, Brick who, dressed in symbolic white silk pyjamas (Edwards), was lost in the illusory world Skipper represented but sprang to life at the very mention of his name (Kemp). The set with bamboo furniture, marble pillars, and swaying chandelier suggested a Delta awash in 'sweaty carnality' (Kemp). Davies's tragi-comic *Cat* ranks as possibly the most powerful production of Williams's play in the UK to date.

A well-received London revival of *Cat* was directed by Arthur Page at the Lyric Theatre in Shaftsbury Avenue, London, on 19 September 2001, and, as we saw, was taken to the United States in 2003. Unlike some earlier American revivals where humour was not a part of Williams's Delta tragedy, Page's stressed the 'Gothic comedy' and the 'supple sinuous nature of [Williams's] prose' (Billington). That 'barbed comedy' came out in exchanges between Brendan Fraser's Brick and Frances O'Connor's Maggie as well as in their caustic attacks on Mae, the children, and Gooper. As Maggie, O'Connor was sexual, witty, but also exhibited the 'frantic restlessness' of a frustrated wife and poverty-fearing daughter-in-law. Taylor found O'Connor 'pent up and wiry . . . a terrific performance'. Even though Fraser's Brick was in his cups, he never lost sight of the mendacity around him, even if at times he was 'bland' (Taylor). His wit, however, was searing, especially in his confrontation with Big Daddy. The 'paradox' of Brick's role for Taylor was that his anger at a 'corrupt society' was 'less a matter of principle than a frightened flight from his own rigid values'. Compared with earlier Big Daddys, the American actor Ned Beatty might not have been as 'earth-

laden', but he nonetheless delivered a resonating performance
as both boss and caring father.

Australia
The first Australian production of *Cat* was at Union Theatre
in Melbourne on 21 October 1957. Union Theatre was run
by the University of Melbourne at the time and became the
precursor of the current Melbourne Theatre Company. Like
premieres in New York and London, *Cat* stirred up controversy
in Australia over its strong sexual content and language.

Productions of Cat *on non-English-speaking stages*
Along with *Streetcar* and *Glass Menagerie*, *Cat on a Hot Tin Roof*
remains one of Williams's most popular plays worldwide.
Within a few months of its American premiere in March 1955,
the Swedish director Ake Falck mounted the first European
production of *Cat* on 2 September at the City Theatre in
Gothenburg. Starring Gunnel Brostrom as Maggie, Herman
Ahlsell as Brick, Karen Kavli as Big Mama, and Kolbjorn
Knudsen as Big Daddy, the play erupted into explosive
confrontations that made it a box-office hit. Later that season,
film and theatre director Ingmar Bergman also staged *Cat*,
with a blond, muscular Max von Sydow as Brick and a portly
Benkt-Ake Benkstsson as Big Daddy. Though he admitted it
was a 'huge success' (*Five O'Clock Angel*, 127), Williams was still
not pleased with the production. Unfortunately, Bergman's *Cat*
did not equal his Swedish premiere of *A Streetcar Named Desire*
six years earlier in Gothenburg (Kolin, *Streetcar*).

The German premiere of *Cat* at Düsseldorf's Schauspielhaus
on 26 November 1955 was heavily cut and bowdlerised (the
elephant joke was omitted as well as numerous stage directions
suggesting sexualised behaviour). Even though the translation
considerably toned down Williams's script, there was 'enough
sexual explicitness left to make the play sensational'. Reviewers
still could still stress, though, that 'voyeurs need not go because
they would not be gratified'. So heavy was Brick's drinking
that Alfons Neukirchen told his readers that after going to *Cat*,

they would not touch a drink for three days'. Contextualising
Cat, some critics diminished the play as a 'cheap dramatization
of the Kinsey report' (Wolter, 17) countering the German
view of America as wholesome and heroic. Even so, the play
remained popular in Germany and Austria. As Sonja Luther
points out, *Cat* saw an unparallelled revival through eight
major productions in Vienna, Hanover, Wiesbaden, Dusseldorf,
Salzburg, etc. during the 2004–5 season. The increased
German interest in *Cat* reflected contemporary political concern,
that is, discontent with America over the Iraq war as well as
dissatisfaction with German politics (Luther, 60). In Andrea
Breth's production in Vienna, for instance, an American flag
was burned on top of Big Daddy's birthday cake. That is not
to say that the sexual elements in *Cat* were censored or
omitted. Burkhard C. Kosminski directed a risqué *Cat* on
24 September 2004 at the Düsseldorf Schauspielhaus, where
Maggie 'walk[ed] around in her panties, bra, and high heels'.

The French premiere of *Cat* on 16 December 1957 at the
Théâtre Antoine, directed by Peter Brook, elicited extremely
angry reviews that faulted Williams for his subject matter and
especially the conclusion of his play (Falb). As their American
counterparts did, French critics found Brick's sexual identity
troubling. Like the Swedish press, too, the French reviewers
found *Cat* far less satisfactory than *Streetcar*. Yet despite such
negative press, *Cat* had a run of 192 performances in Paris.

Not surprisingly, *Cat* did not come to Communist countries
until many years after its New York premiere. *Cat* was not
staged in the USSR until December 1981, twelve years after
the Soviets had seen *Streetcar* and *Glass Menagerie*. No doubt the
Soviet censors, like their American counterparts three decades
earlier, were troubled by the play's strong sexual content,
particularly its references to homosexuality. When *Cat* did
open at the Mayakovsky Theatre in Moscow, the Soviet
director in all likelihood received permission to stage the play
'to expose the degradation and decadence of the bourgeoise
world' (Schmemann). Nonetheless, Soviet audiences responded
positively to Williams's play and saw numerous comparisons
between his work and Chekhov's – in tone, characterisation,
and plot (the fragmentation of the family and the questions

over inheritance). The Russian translator proclaimed that Williams was 'the biggest success since Chekhov' (quoted in Schmemann). This reaction is not surprising given Williams's life-long indebtedness to Chekhov, even adapting *The Seagull* (1896) in his *The Notebook of Trigorin* in 1981.

In May 1987, the Shanghai University Drama Institute staged a stirring *Cat on a Hot Tin Roof* (rendered *Cat on a Hot Iron Roof*), which may have been the earliest professional production of Williams's play in Communist China (Kolin and Shao 19).

Adaptations of *Cat* for film and TV

The film adaptation (1958)

Three years after the Broadway premiere, MGM released the film adaptation of *Cat* in 1958. A huge box-office hit grossing ten million dollars in the US alone, *Cat* was the most commercially successful film of any Williams play. Using the Kazan-influenced Broadway script, the director Richard Brooks (who in 1962 directed the film version of *Sweet Bird of Youth*) and James Poe co-wrote the MGM screenplay (108 minutes). The film featured two sky-rocketing stars – Paul Newman as the arrogant, sullen, non-conformist Brick, a character type he would develop more fully in *Cool Hand Luke* and *The Hustler*, and a sensual, kittenish, yet aggressive twenty-six-year-old Elizabeth Taylor as Maggie who later played the seductive and wily queen in *Cleopatra* (1964). Together they carried audiences into the steamy world of passion that the trailers promised. Posters in the UK and America showed Taylor lying, longingly, on a big brass bed or peering, like a prisoner, between the bars of the headboard, begging for sexual satisfaction. Reprising his Broadway role as Big Daddy, Burl Ives again won raves for his boisterous interpretation, but he got much closer to his estranged son Brick in the film than he did in Williams's play. The film was nominated for six Oscars but, unfortunately, did not win any.

The MGM *Cat* was a provocative film in 1958, and even today retains sensational qualities. The reviewer for *Harrison's Report* observed, 'Some slight and necessary changes have been made in the story to clean it up for the film version, but the considerable talk about sex is as frank and forthright as anything ever heard in a motion picture' (quoted in Palmer and Bray, 174–5). Brooks was faced with the thorny problem of sanitising Williams's script while still being faithful to his intentions. To accommodate Hollywood censors, and pass the Production Code, Brooks severely muted or veiled any references to homosexuality. Brick's major problem in the film was not his sexual identity but his estrangement from Big Daddy (Spoto, 'Commentary'). Family problems became the leading theme in the film version of *Cat*.

While Skipper does not appear in Brooks's film, he was nevertheless transformed from the closet gay into the unrepentant stud. Audiences are led to believe that Maggie tried to seduce or was nearly seduced by Brick's best friend. Going to Skipper's hotel room, she reports to Brick: 'He kissed me. That was the first time he'd ever touched me. And then I knew what I was gonna do. I'd get rid of Skipper. I'd show Brick that their deep true friendship was a big lie. I'd provide it by showin' that Skipper would make love to the wife of his best friend. He didn't need any coaxin'. He was more than willin'. He even seemed to have the same idea.' Maggie then tells Brick that 'Skipper was no good' and that 'Without you Skipper was nothing'. Celebrating heterosexual marriage, the film supplied a conventional Hollywood happy ending. Brick hobbles upstairs to the bedroom, and insists that Maggie join him. To which Taylor's Maggie confidently, and loudly, sounds off, 'Yes, sir.' The film closes with Taylor at the bedroom door as Brick declares, 'Maggie, we are through with lies and liars in this house. Lock the door.' Brooks left no doubt that Maggie's 'lie' will come true. While Brooks created a box-office sensation, Williams claimed that the film was not faithful to his characterisation of Brick and Maggie.

Although Brooks made substantial changes to Williams's play, he nevertheless built upon its formidable cinematic qualities. Consistent with MGM's action-packed films, he opened *Cat* up by including several new sets where we hear Hollywood dialogue and witness additional action. A pre-opening scene shows a drunken Brick jumping hurdles in the dark at his high school athletic field to the sound of cheering crowds, but when he stumbles and breaks his ankle, the camera pans to an empty, silent stadium. From Brick's midnight run, *Cat* moves to the airfield where Big Daddy returns home from the Oschner clinic and is driven by Maggie to his mansion via his horse farm. His birthday dinner is outside on the lawn, complete with the caterwauling of Gooper's no-neck offspring. After telling Big Daddy the truth in Act Two, Brick tries to leave the estate, but his car gets stuck in the mud on a stormy night; he sits in an open convertible, rain pelting him until Maggie comes to the rescue. In Act Three, Brooks moves to the basement of the mansion where, amid cobwebs hanging over the Pollitt's possessions, an emotional conversation occurs between father and son. Retreating there to kill his pain with booze, but refusing the injection that Brick wants to administer, Big Daddy bonds with his son, asking, 'Why didn't you come to me . . . and not Skipper?' To which Newman's Brick confesses, 'All I wanted was a father, not a boss.' Brooks makes a powerful statement about Brick's destructive self-image and his failed relationship with Big Daddy when Newman tears apart a large poster of him in his college football uniform hanging on the basement wall.

TV adaptations

A trendy made-for-TV *Cat on a Hot Tin Roof*, produced by Laurence Olivier, appeared on NBC TV, 6 December 1976. Although Olivier attempted to restore Williams's original script, his *Cat* had to be trimmed into six short scenes (100 minutes) to accommodate commercials, lessening the emotional effect of the play. According to Hal Erickson, Olivier's production was 'more sexually explicit than the censor-driven 1958 Hollywood version, but [it] wasn't quite as strong dramatically despite its powerhouse cast'. Olivier's Big Daddy was very different from Burl Ives's interpretation of the role. Dressed in a tailored white linen suit and with his coiffed white hair and moustache, Olivier looked more like a stately elder Mark Twain or slimmer Colonel Sanders projecting an aristocratic Big Daddy, not the self-made, coarse

man Williams imagined. According to John O'Connor,
Olivier's Big Daddy 'has been artistically castrated. His language
has been toned down, his off-color jokes have been eliminated,
his incorrigible lustfulness has been diluted' (D: 29). Big
Daddy's plantation, too, underwent remodelling. In Olivier's
version, it became an elegant mansion with exquisite furniture,
crystal chandeliers, and white-jacketed servants evoking the
lavish homes in such TV epics as *Dallas* or *Dynasty*.

The husband-and-wife team of Natalie Wood and Robert
Wagner were (mis)cast as Maggie and Brick. While critics
praised Wood for her sensuality and sincerity; O'Connor,
however, faulted her for 'wielding a cigarette, [that] seems to
be offering a campy imitation of Bette Davis'. Wagner was
not up to the role and was compared to a soap-opera actor.
At forty-six, he was older and less passionate than Newman's
thirtyish Brick. Regrettably, there were few sparks in his
conversations with Maggie. Moreover, his confrontations with
Olivier were tepid compared to Newman's with Ives's
Big Daddy. As if symbolising his indolence, Wagner's Brick
languished in a Victorian-era bath tub, a drink in his hand
and his leg, in a partial cast, hanging over the side.

A second made-for-TV *Cat* premiered on Showtime on 19
August 1984 and was re-broadcast on 24 June 1985 on PBS as
part of the American Playhouse series. Using the uncensored
text of *Cat* (1975), this televised version was classified as
'Family Drama', Psychological Drama', and 'Melodrama'.
Directed by Jack Hofsiss (*Elephant Man*), the 1984 televised
Cat was an improvement over Olivier's but still 'flounder[ed]'
because of miscasting and misguided acting. According to
O'Connor, Tommy Lee Jones (Brick) 'feels as though he is
acting with a muzzle on'; his Brick was so forlorn, so removed
from Maggie that there could be 'no ambiguity' about any
future with her. While Jessica Lange portrayed Maggie's
beauty and sensuality, she was 'curiously distant', behaving as
if 'she hasn't been introduced to the rest of the cast'. A cool
Brick works; a cool Maggie 'disables' the play. Lange made a
better Blanche DuBois (2004) than she did a Maggie. Rip
Torn's Big Daddy, however, received high marks for his
intensity, and his interactions with Jones marked the highlight

of the televised version, as in so many stage productions of *Cat*. But Torn's thick Southern accent was sometimes hard to understand. Kim Stanley, who played Maggie in the British premiere, brought an unexpected shrewdness to the role of Big Mama. Yet even with this star power, this televised *Cat* could not measure up to Williams's script.

Further Reading

Selected plays by Williams

The Theatre of Tennessee Williams, vol.1: *Battle of Angels, The Glass Menagerie, A Streetcar Named Desire*. New York: New Directions, 1971

The Theatre of Tennessee Williams, vol. 2: *The Eccentricities of a Nightingale, Summer and Smoke, The Rose Tattoo, Camino Real*. New York: New Directions, 1976

The Theatre of Tennessee Williams, vol. 3: *Cat on a Hot Tin Roof, Orpheus Descending, Suddenly Last Summer*. New York: New Directions, 1971

The Theatre of Tennessee Williams, vol. 4: *Sweet Bird of Youth, Period of Adjustment, The Night of the Iguana*. New York: New Directions, 1972

The Glass Menagerie. London: Methuen, 2000

Not About Nightingales. London: Methuen, 1998

Spring Storm. New York: New Directions, 1999

Stairs to the Roof. New York: New Directions, 2000

A Streetcar Named Desire. London: Methuen, 1984; reissued 2009

Selected prose, poetry and essays by Williams

The Collected Poems of Tennessee Williams, ed. David Roessel and Nicholas Moschovakis. New York: New Directions, 2002

Collected Stories. New York: New Directions, 1994

'Critic Says "Evasion", Writer Says "Mystery",' *Tennessee Williams: New Selected Essays: Where I Live*, ed. John S. Bak, New York: New Directions, 2009, 76–8.

Memoirs. New York: Doubleday, 1975

Moise and the World of Reason. New York: Simon and Schuster, 1975

Notebooks: Tennessee Williams, ed. Margaret Bradham Thornton. New Haven: Yale UP, 2006

'Notes to the Reader', *Tennessee Williams: New Selected Essays: Where I Live*, ed. John S. Bak. New York: New Directions, 2009, 25–7

The Roman Spring of Mrs Stone. London: Vintage, 1999

'Something Wild . . . ', *Tennessee Williams: New Selected Essays: Where I Live*, ed. John S. Bak. New York: New Directions, 2009, 43–8

Books on Williams and American drama

Adler, Thomas P., *Mirror on the Stage: The Pulitzer Prize Play as an Approach to American Drama*. West Lafayette, IN: Purdue UP, 1987

Bigsby, C.W.E., *A Critical Introduction to Twentieth-Century American Drama, vol. 2: Williams, Miller, Albee*. Cambridge: Cambridge UP, 1984

Clum, John, *Acting Gay: Male Homosexuality in American Drama*. New York: Columbia University Press, 1992

Donkin, Ellen, and Susan Clement (eds), *Upstaging Big Daddy: Direct Theatre as if Gender and Race Matter*. Ann Arbor: University of Michigan Press, 1993

Kolin, Philip C., *The Tennessee Williams Encyclopedia*. Westport, CT: Greenwood Press, 2004

———, *Tennessee Williams: A Guide to Research and Performance*. Westport, CT: Greenwood Press, 1988

———, *Williams: A Streetcar Named Desire. Plays in Production*. Cambridge: Cambridge UP, 2000

——— and Colby H. Kullman (eds), *Speaking on Stage: Interviews with Contemporary American Playwrights*. Tuscaloosa: University of Alabama Press, 1996

Leverich, Lyle, *Tom: The Unknown Tennessee Williams*. New York: Crown, 1995

Mitgang, Herbert, *Dangerous Dossiers: Exposing the Secret War Against America's Greatest Authors*. New York: Ballantine, 1988

Murphy, Brenda, *Tennessee Williams and Elia Kazan: A Collaboration in the Theatre*. Cambridge: Cambridge UP, 1992

Paller, Michael, *Gentlemen Callers: Tennessee Williams, Homosexuality, and Mid-Twentieth-Century Broadway Drama*. New York, Palgrave, 2005

Palmer, R. Barton, and William Robert Bray, *Hollywood's Tennessee: The Williams Films and Postwar America*. Austin: University of Texas Press, 2009

Saddik, Annette, *The Politics of Reputation: The Critical Perception of Tennessee Williams' Later Plays*, London: Associated University Press, 1998

St Just, Maria, *Five O'Clock Angel: Letters of Tennessee Williams to Maria St Just*. New York: Penguin, 1990

Savran, David, *Cowboys, Communists, and Queers: The Politics of Masculinity in the Work of Arthur Miller and Tennessee Williams*. Minneapolis: University of Minnesota Press, 1992

Spoto, Donald, *The Kindness of Strangers: The Life of Tennessee Williams*. Boston: Little, Brown, 1985

Thompson, Judith, *Tennessee Williams's Plays: Memory, Myth, and Symbol*. New York: Peter Lang, 1989

Tischler, Nancy, *Tennessee Williams: Rebellious Puritan*. New York: Citadel, 1961

Articles on *Cat on a Hot Tin Roof*

Arrell, Douglas, 'Homosexual Panic in *Cat on a Hot Tin Roof*', *Modern Drama* 51 (Spring 2008): 60–72

Bak, John S., ' "Sneakin' and spyin' " from Broadway to the Beltway: Cold War Masculinity, Brick, and Homosexual Existentialism'. *Theatre Journal* 56 (2004): 225–49

Bibler, Michael P., ' "A Tenderness which was Uncommon": Homosexuality, Narrative, and the Southern Plantation in Tennessee Williams's *Cat on a Hot Tin Roof*'. *Mississippi Quarterly* 55 (Summer 2002): 381–400

Canadas, Ivan, 'The Naming of Jack Straw and Peter Ochello in Tennessee Williams's *Cat on a Hot Tin Roof*'. *English Language Notes* 42 (June 2005): 57–62

Crandell, George, 'Echo Spring: Reflecting the Gaze of Narcissus in Tennessee Williams's *Cat on a Hot Tin Roof*'. *Modern Drama* 42 (Autumn 1999): 427–41

Devlin, Albert J., 'Writing in "A Place of Stone": *Cat on a Hot Tin Roof*'. *The Cambridge Companion to Tennessee Williams*, ed. Matthew C. Roudané. Cambridge: Cambridge UP, 1997, 95–113

Dukore, Bernard F., 'The Cat Has Nine Lives'. *TDR* 8 (Autumn 1963): 95–100

Gross, Robert F., 'The Pleasures of Brick: Eros and the Gay Spectator in *Cat on a Hot Tin Roof*'. *Journal of American Drama and Theater* 9.1 (1997): 11–25

Hale, Allean, 'How a Tiger Became the Cat'. *Tennessee Williams Literary Journal* 2.1 (Winter 1990–91): 33–6

Hurd, Myles Raymond, 'Cats and Catamites: Patroclus and Williams's *Cat on a Hot Tin Roof*'. *Notes on Mississippi Writers* 23 (1991): 63–5

Isaac, Dan, 'Big Daddy's Dramatic Word Strings'. *American Speech* 40 (Dec. 1965): 272–8

Kolin, Philip C., 'Obstacles to Communication in *Cat on a Hot Tin Roof*'. *Western Speech Communication* 39 (1975): 74–80
———, 'Williams's *Cat on a Hot Tin Roof*'. *The Explicator* 50.4 (Summer 2002): 214–15

Kullman, Colby H., 'Rule by Power: "Big Daddyism" in the World of Tennessee Williams's Plays'. *Mississippi Quarterly* 48 (Autumn 1995): 667–76

May, Charles, 'Brick Pollitt as Homo Ludens: "Three Players of a Summer Game" and *Cat on a Hot Tin Roof*'. *Tennessee Williams: A Tribute*, ed. Jac Tharpe. Jackson: UP of Mississippi, 1977, 277–91

Mayberry, Susan Neal, 'A Study of Illusion and the Grotesque in Tennessee Williams's *Cat on a Hot Tin Roof*'. *Southern Studies* 22 (1983): 359–65

Parker, Brian, 'Swinging a Cat' in *Cat on a Hot Tin Roof*. New York: New Directions, 2004. 175–86

Shackelford, Dean, 'The Truth that Must Be Told: Gay Subjectivity, Homophobia, and Social History in *Cat on a Hot Tin Roof*'. *Tennessee Williams Annual Review* 1 (1998): 103–8

Thornton, Margaret Bradham, 'Between the Lines: Editing the *Notebooks* of Tennessee Williams'. *Theatre History Studies* 28 (2008): 7–20

Walters, Arthur, 'Tennessee Williams: Ten Years Later'. *Theatre Arts*, July 1958: 742–3

Winchell, Mark Royden, 'Come Back to the Locker Room Ag'in, Brick Honey!' *Mississippi Quarterly* 48 (Autumn 1995): 701–12

Production reviews

Broadway premiere, 1955

Atkinson, Brooks, 'Theatre: Tennessee Williams's *Cat*'. *New York Times* 25 March 1955: 18; reprinted *New York Theatre Critics' Reviews* 16 (1955): 344

Bentley, Eric, '*Cat on a Hot Tin Roof*'. *New Republic*, 11 April 1955. 28–9

Chapman, John, '*Cat on a Hot Tin Roof* Beautifully Acted, but a Frustrating Drama'. *New York Daily News*, 25 March 1955: 65; reprinted *New York Theatre Critics' Reviews* 16 (1955): 343

Coleman, Robert, "*Cat on a Hot Tin Roof* Is Likely to Be a Hit". *New York Daily Mirror*, 25 March 1955; reprinted *New York Theatre Critics' Reviews* 16 (1955): 342

Hawkins, William, 'Cat Yowls High on "Hot Tin Roof".' *New York World-Telegram*, 25 March 1955; reprinted *New York Theatre Critics' Reviews* 16 (1955): 342

Kerr, Walter F., '*Cat on a Hot Tin Roof*'. *New York Herald Tribune*, 25 March 1955: 12; reprinted *New York Theatre Critics' Reviews* 16 (1955): 342

McClain, John, 'Drama Socks and Shocks'. *New York Journal-American*, 25 March 1955: 20; reprinted *New York Theatre Critics' Reviews* 16 (1955): 344

Watts, Richard, Jr., 'The Impact of Tennessee Williams'. *New York Post*, 25 March 1955: 57; reprinted in *New York Theatre Critics' Reviews* 16 (1955): 343–4

USA, 1974

Barnes, Clive, *New York Times*, 25 September 1974: 26; reprinted *New York Theatre Critics' Reviews* 35 (1974): 242

Kalem, T. E., *Time*, 7 October 1974: 107

Probst, Leonard, '*Cat*', NBC Radio, 25 September 1974; reprinted *New York Theatre Critics' Reviews* 35 (1974): 246

Sharp, Christopher, *Women's Wear Daily*, 25 September 1974; reprinted *New York Theatre Critics' Reviews* 35 (1974): 244

Snyder, Louis, *Christian Science Monitor*, 27 September 1974; reprinted in *New York Theatre Critics' Reviews* 35 (1974): 244–5

Wilson, Edwin, *Wall Street Journal*, 27 Sept. 1974; reprinted
    New York Theatre Critics' Reviews 35 (1974): 243–4

USA, 1990

Barnes, Clive, *New York Post*, 22 March 1990; reprinted *New
    York Theatre Critics' Reviews* 51 (1990): 353–4
Henry, William A., *Time*, 2 April 1990: 71–2; reprinted *New
    York Theatre Critics' Reviews* 51 (1990): 357
Kroll, Jack, *Newsweek*, 2 April 1990: 54; reprinted *New York
    Theatre Critics' Reviews* 51 (1990): 355
Rich, Frank, *New York Times*, 22 March 1990: 81; reprinted
    New York Theatre Critics' Reviews 51 (1990): 356–7
Siegel, Joel J., WABC TV, 21 March 1990; reprinted *New York
    Theatre Critics' Reviews* 51 (1990): 359
Wilson, Edwin, *Wall Street Journal*, 26 March 1990; reprinted
    New York Theatre Critics' Reviews 51 (1990): 356
Winer, Linda, 'In *Cat*, It's Kathleen's Show'. *New York Newsday*,
    22 March 1990; reprinted *New York Theatre Critics' Reviews*
    51 (1990): 358

USA, 2003

Brantley, Ben, 'Big Daddy's Ego Defies Death and His Family'.
    New York Times, 3 November, 2003
Kissel, Howard, '*Cat* – Down Home Southern Hostility'. *New
    York Daily News*, 3 November 2003
Lahr, John, 'Bitches and Witches: Ulterior Motives in *Cat on a
    Hot Tin Roof* and *Wicked*', *New Yorker*, 10 November 2003
Murray, Matthew, 'Broadway Reviews: *Cat on a Hot Tin Roof*'.
    talkinbroadway.com, 6 March 2003
Schwarzbaum, Lisa, 'Meow Mix'. *Variety*, 2 November 2003
Sommer, Elyse, 'Curtain Up Review of *Cat*'
    http://www.curtainup.com/catonahottinroof.html

USA, 2008

Barnes, Clive, 'Roof' Is the Cat's Meow', *New York Post*,
    7 March 2008
———, '*Cat* Lives Up to Its Expectations'. stereohyped.com

Brantley, Ben, 'Yet Another Life for Maggie'. *New York Times*, 7
    March 2008

Denton, Martin, '*Cat*'. *nytheatre.com review*, 13 March 2008

Dziemianowicz, J., 'Only James Earl Jones'. *New York Daily
    News*, 7 March 2008

Fisher, Luchina, 'Is Broadway Going Black?' ABC News,
    1 May 2008

Portantiere, Michael, Review of *Cat*. http://AfterElton.
    com/theatre/2008/catonahottinroof.htm

Robertson, Campbell, 'A Black *Cat*, Catching an Elusive
    Audience'. *New York Times*, 20 March 2008

Teachout, Terry, '*Cat* Freshly Skinned', *Wall Street Journal*,
    7 March 2008: W9

UK, 1958

'*Cat on a Hot Tin Roof*', *The Times* (London): 31 January 1958: 3

'London Sees *Cat*, Opinion is Divided'. *New York Times*, 31
    January 1958: 21

Tynan, Kenneth, *Curtains*. New York: Atheneum, 1961: 202–4

UK, 1988

Billington, Michael, '*Cat on a Hot Tin Roof.*' *Guardian*,
    4 February 1988; reprinted *London Theatre Record* 1988: 135

Edwards, Christopher, '*Cat on a Hot Tin Roof*'. *Spectator*, 20
    February 1988; reprinted *London Theatre Record* 8 1988:136

Kemp, Peter B., '*Cat on a Hot Tin Roof*'. *Independent*, 4 February
    1988; reprinted *London Theatre Record* 1988:134

King, Francis, '*Cat on a Hot Tin Roof*'. *Sunday Telegraph*, 7
    February 1988; reprinted *London Theatre Record* 1988:138

Radin, Victoria, '*Cat on a Hot Tin Roof*'. *New Statesman*, 19
    February 1988; reprinted *London Theatre Record* 1988:137

Ratcliffe, Michael, '*Cat on a Hot Tin Roof*'. *Observer*, 7 February
    1988; reprinted *London Theatre Record* 1988:139–40

UK, 2001

Billington, Michael, '*Cat*'. *Guardian*, 19 September 2001

Taylor, S., 'The Claws are Still Sharp'. *Independent*, 20 September 2001

China

Kolin, Philip, and Shao, Sherry, 'The First *Streetcar* in Mainland China'. *Tennessee Williams Literary Journal* 2 no. 1 (Winter 1990–1): 19–32

France

Falb, Lewis W., *American Drama in Paris: 1945–1970. A Study of Its Critical Reception*. Chapel Hill: University of North Carolina Press, 1973

Germany

Luther, Sonja, 'German Translations and Performances of Tennessee Williams's *A Streetcar Named Desire* and *Cat on Hot Tin Roof*: 1955 Until 2005'. MA thesis. University of Southern Mississippi, August 2007

Wolter, Jürgen, 'Tennessee Williams in Germany'. *Tennessee Williams Literary Journal* 3 (1995): 9–13

Russia

Schmemann, Serge, 'The Russian Theatregoers Take Tennessee Williams to Their Hearts'. *New York Times*, 31 December 1981

Sweden

Gint, Dirk, 'Torn between "Swedish Sin" and "Homosexual Freemasonry": Tennessee Williams, sexual morals and the closet in 1950s Sweden'. *Tennessee Williams Annual Review* 11 (2010)

Film, 1958

Palmer, R. Barton and Bray, William Robert, *Hollywood's Tennessee: The Williams Films and Postwar America.* Austin: University of Texas Press, 2009

Spoto, Donald, 'Commentary'. *Cat on a Hot Tin Roof* (DVD.) Warner Home Video. Burbank, CA., 2004

TV, 1976

Erikson, Hal, *Cat.* All Movie Guide, movies.msn.com

O'Connor, John, 'The Tribute Smacks of Exploitation'. *New York Times*, 5 December 1976: D29

TV, 1984

O'Connor, John, 'From Cable to Air: *Cat*', *New York Times*, 24 June 1985

Cat on a Hot Tin Roof

And you, my father, there on the sad height,
Curse, bless, me now with your fierce tears, I pray.
Do not go gentle into that good night.
Rage, rage against the dying of the light.

Dylan Thomas

For Maria

Cat on a Hot Tin Roof was originally presented at the Morosco Theatre in New York on 24 March 1955, starring Barbara Bel Geddes, Ben Gazzara, Mildred Dunnock and Burl Ives, directed by Elia Kazan.

Cat on a Hot Tin Roof was restaged by the American Shakespeare Theatre in Stratford, Connecticut, with the third act rewritten, along with other substantial revisions, on 10 July 1974. That version of the play, which is printed here, reopened in New York on 24 September 1974 at the ANTA Theatre. Both 1974 productions were directed by Michael Kahn, designed by John Conklin, with lighting by Marc B. Weiss, and costumes by Jane Greenwood. The cast was as follows:

Margaret	Elizabeth Ashley
Brick	Keir Dullea
Dixie	Deborah Grove
Mae	Joan Pape
Gooper	Charles Siebert
Big Mama	Kate Reid
Sookey	Saraellen
Big Daddy	Fred Gwyne
Reverend Tooker	Wyman Pendleton
Doctor Baugh	William Larsen
Lacey*	Thomas Anderson
Children*	Jeb Brown
	Chris Browning
	Betsy Spivak
	Susannah Brown

* In the New York production, the part of Lacey was not included, and the number of children was reduced to three, played by Jeb Brown, Sukie Brown and Amy Borress.

Characters

Margaret
Brick
Dixie, *a little girl*
Mae, *sometimes called Sister Woman*
Gooper, *sometimes called Brother Man*
Big Mama
Sookey, *a Negro servant*
Big Daddy
Reverend Tooker
Doctor Baugh, *pronounced 'Baw'*
Lacey, *a Negro servant*
Children

Notes for the Designer

The set is the bed-sitting-room of a plantation home in the Mississippi Delta. It is along an upstairs gallery which probably runs around the entire house; it has two pairs of very wide doors opening onto the gallery, showing white balustrades against a fair summer sky that fades into dusk and night during the course of the play, which occupies precisely the time of its performance, excepting, of course, the fifteen minutes of intermission.

Perhaps the style of the room is not what you would expect in the home of the Delta's biggest cotton-planter. It is Victorian with a touch of the Far East. It hasn't changed much since it was occupied by the original owners of the place, Jack Straw and Peter Ochello, a pair of old bachelors who shared this room all their lives together. In other words, the room must evoke some ghosts; it is gently and poetically haunted by a relationship that must have involved a tenderness which was uncommon. This may be irrelevant or unnecessary, but I once saw a reproduction of a faded photograph of the verandah of Robert Louis Stevenson's home on that Samoan Island where he spent his last years, and there was a quality of tender light on weathered wood, such as porch furniture made of bamboo and wicker, exposed to tropical suns and tropical rains, which came to mind when I thought about the set for this play, bringing also to mind the grace and comfort of light, the reassurance it gives, on a late and fair afternoon in summer, the way that no matter what, even dread of death is gently touched and soothed by it. For the set is the background for a play that deals with human extremities of emotion, and it needs that softness behind it.

The bathroom door, showing only pale-blue tile and silver towel racks, is in one side wall; the hall door in the opposite wall. Two articles of furniture need mention: a big double bed which staging should make a functional part of the set as often as suitable, the surface of which should be slightly raked to make figures on it seen more easily; and against the wall space between the two huge double doors upstage: a monumental monstrosity peculiar to our times, a *huge* console combination of radio-phonograph (hi-fi with three speakers) TV set *and* liquor cabinet, bearing and containing many glasses and bottles, all in one piece, which is a composition of muted silver tones, and the opalescent tones of reflecting glass, a chromatic link, this thing, between the sepia (tawny gold) tones of the interior and the cool (white and blue) tones of the gallery and sky. This piece of furniture (?!), this monument, is a very complete and compact little shrine to virtually all the comforts and illusions behind which we hide from such things as the characters in the play are faced with . . .

The set should be far less realistic than I have so far implied in this description of it. I think the walls below the ceiling should dissolve mysteriously into air; the set should be roofed by the sky; stars and moon suggested by traces of milky pallor, as if they were observed through a telescope lens out of focus.

Anything else I can think of? Oh, yes, fanlights (transoms shaped like an open glass fan) above all the doors in the set, with panes of blue and amber, and above all, the designer should take as many pains to give the actors room to move about freely (to show their restlessness, their passion for breaking out) as if it were a set for a ballet.

An evening in summer. The action is continuous, with two intermissions.

Act One

At the rise of the curtain someone is taking a shower in the bathroom, the door of which is half open. A pretty young woman, with anxious lines in her face, enters the bedroom and crosses to the bathroom door.

Margaret (*shouting above roar of water*)   One of those no-neck monsters hit me with a hot buttered biscuit so I have t' change!

Margaret's voice is both rapid and drawling. In her long speeches she has the vocal tricks of a priest delivering a liturgical chant, the lines are almost sung, always continuing a little beyond her breath so she has to gasp for another. Sometimes she intersperses the lines with a little wordless singing, such as 'Da-da-daaaa!'

Water turns off and **Brick** *calls out to her, but is still unseen. A tone of politely feigned interest, masking indifference, or worse, is characteristic of his speech with* **Margaret**.

Brick   Wha'd you say, Maggie? Water was on s' loud I couldn't hearya . . .

Margaret   Well, I! – just remarked that! – one of th' no-neck monsters messed up m' lovely lace dress so I got t' – cha-a-ange . . .

She opens and kicks shut drawers of the dresser.

Brick   Why d'ya call Gooper's kiddies no-neck monsters?

Margaret   Because they've got no necks! Isn't that a good enough reason?

Brick   Don't they have any necks?

Margaret   None visible. Their fat little heads are set on their fat little bodies without a bit of connection.

Brick   That's too bad.

Margaret   Yes, it's too bad because you can't wring their necks if they've got no necks to wring! Isn't that right, honey?

She steps out of her dress, stands in a slip of ivory satin and lace.

Yép, they're no-neck monsters, all no-neck people are
monsters . . .

Children shriek downstairs.

Hear them? Hear them screaming? I don't know where their
voice boxes are located since they don't have necks. I tell you I
got so nervous at that table tonight I thought I would throw
back my head and utter a scream you could hear across the
Arkansas border an' parts of Louisiana an' Tennessee. I said to
your charming sister-in-law, Mae, honey, couldn't you feed
those precious little things at a separate table with an oilcloth
cover? They make such a mess an' the lace cloth looks *so*
pretty! She made enormous eyes at me and said, 'Ohhh,
noooooo! On Big Daddy's birthday? Why, he would never
forgive me!' Well, I want you to know, Big Daddy hadn't been
at the table two minutes with those five no-neck monsters
slobbering and drooling over their food before he threw down
his fork an' shouted, 'Fo' God's sake, Gooper, why don't you
put them pigs at a trough in th' kitchen?' – Well, I swear, I
simply could have di-ieed!

Think of it, Brick, they've got five of them and number six is
coming. They've brought the whole bunch down here like
animals to display at a county fair. Why, they have those
children doin' tricks all the time! 'Junior, show Big Daddy how
you do this, show Big Daddy how you do that, say your little
piece fo' Big Daddy, Sister. Show your dimples, Sugar. Brother,
show Big Daddy how you stand on your head!' – It goes on all
the time, along with constant little remarks and innuendos
about the fact that you and I have not produced any children,
are totally childless and therefore totally useless! – Of course
it's comical but it's also disgusting since it's so obvious what
they're up to!

Brick (*without interest*) What are they up to, Maggie?

Margaret Why, you know what they're up to!

Brick (*appearing*) No, I don't know what they're up to.

He stands there in the bathroom doorway drying his hair with a towel and hanging onto the towel rack because one ankle is broken, plastered and bound. He is still slim and firm as a boy. His liquor hasn't started tearing him down outside. He has the additional charm of that cool air of detachment that people have who have given up the struggle. But now and then, when disturbed, something flashes behind it, like lightning in a fair sky, which shows that at some deeper level he is far from peaceful. Perhaps in a stronger light he would show some signs of deliquescence, but the fading, still warm, light from the gallery treats him gently.

Margaret   I'll tell you what they're up to, boy of mine! –
They're up to cutting you out of your father's estate, and –

She freezes momentarily before her next remark. Her voice drops as if it were somehow a personally embarrassing admission.

– Now we know that Big Daddy's dyin' of – *cancer* . . .

There are voices on the lawn below: long-drawn calls across distance.
Margaret *raises her lovely bare arms and powders her armpits with a light sigh.*

She adjusts the angle of a magnifying mirror to straighten an eyelash, then rises fretfully saying:

There's so much light in the room it –

Brick (*softly but sharply*)   Do we?

Margaret   Do we what?

Brick   Know Big Daddy's dyin' of cancer?

Margaret   Got the report today.

Brick   Oh . . .

Margaret (*letting down bamboo blinds which cast long, gold-fretted shadows over the room*)   Yep, got th' report just now . . . it didn't surprise me, Baby.

Her voice has range, and music; sometimes it drops low as a boy's and you have a sudden image of her playing boy's games as a child.

I recognized the symptoms soon's we got here last spring and I'm willin' to bet you that Brother Man and his wife were pretty sure of it, too. That more than likely explains why their usual summer migration to the coolness of the Great Smokies was passed up this summer in favor of – hustlin' down here ev'ry whipstitch with their whole screamin' tribe! And why so many allusions have been made to Rainbow Hill lately. You know what Rainbow Hill is? Place that's famous for treatin' alcoholics an' dope fiends in the movies!

Brick   I'm not in the movies.

Margaret   No, and you don't take dope. Otherwise you're a perfect candidate for Rainbow Hill, Baby, and that's where they aim to ship you – over my dead body! Yep, over my dead body they'll ship you there, but nothing would please them better. Then Brother Man could get a-hold of the purse strings and dole out remittances to us, maybe get power of attorney and sign checks for us and cut off our credit wherever, whenever he wanted! Son-of-a-bitch! – How'd you like that, Baby? Well, you've been doin' just about ev'rything in your power to bring it about, you've just been doin' ev'rything you can think of to aid and abet them in this scheme of theirs! Quittin' work, devoting yourself to the occupation of drinkin'! – Breakin' your ankle last night on the high school athletic field: doin' what? Jumpin' hurdles? At two or three in the morning? Just fantastic! Got in the paper. *Clarksdale Register* carried a nice little item about it, human interest story about a well-known former athlete stagin' a one-man track meet on the Glorious Hill High School athletic field last night, but was slightly out of condition and didn't clear the first hurdle! Brother Man Gooper claims he exercised his influence t' keep it from goin' out over AP or UP or every goddam 'P'.

But, Brick? You still have one big advantage!

During the above swift flood of words, **Brick** *has reclined with contrapuntal leisure on the snowy surface of the bed and has rolled over carefully on his side or belly.*

Brick (*wryly*)   Did you *say* something, Maggie?

Margaret   Big Daddy dotes on you, honey. And he can't stand Brother Man and Brother Man's wife, that monster of

fertility, Mae. Know how I know? By little expressions that
flicker over his face when that woman is holding fo'th on one
of her choice topics such as − how she refused twilight sleep! −
when the twins were delivered! Because she feels motherhood's
an experience that a woman ought to experience fully! − in
order to fully appreciate the wonder and beauty of it! HAH! −
and how she made Brother Man come in an' stand beside her
in the delivery room so he would not miss out on the 'wonder
and beauty' of it either! − producin' those no-neck monsters . . .

A speech of this kind would be antipathetic from almost anybody but
Margaret; *she makes it oddly funny, because her eyes constantly
twinkle and her voice shakes with laughter which is basically indulgent.*

− Big Daddy shares my attitude toward those two! As for me,
well − I give him a laugh now and then and he tolerates me. In
fact! − I sometimes suspect that Big Daddy harbors a little
unconscious 'lech' fo' me . . .

Brick   What makes you think that Big Daddy has a lech for
you, Maggie?

Margaret   Way he always drops his eyes down my body
when I'm talkin' to him, drops his eyes to my boobs an' licks
his old chops! Ha ha!

Brick   That kind of talk is disgusting.

Margaret   Did anyone ever tell you that you're an ass-aching
Puritan, Brick?

I think it's mighty fine that that ole fellow, on the doorstep of
death, still takes in my shape with what I think is deserved
appreciation!

And you wanta know something else? Big Daddy didn't know
how many little Maes and Goopers had been produced! 'How
many kids have you got?' he asked at the table, just like Brother
Man and his wife were new acquaintances to him! Big Mama
said he was jokin', but that ole boy wasn't jokin', Lord, no!

And when they infawmed him that they had five already and were turning out number six! – the news seemed to come as a sort of unpleasant surprise . . .

Children yell below.

Scream, monsters!

Turns to **Brick** *with a sudden, gay, charming smile which fades as she notices that he is not looking at her but into fading gold space with a troubled expression.*

It is constant rejection that makes her humor 'bitchy'.

Margaret   Yes, you should of been at that supper-table, Baby.

Whenever she calls him 'baby' the word is a soft caress.

Y'know, Big Daddy, bless his ole sweet soul, he's the dearest ole thing in the world, but he does hunch over his food as if he preferred not to notice anything else. Well, Mae an' Gooper were side by side at the table, direckly across from Big Daddy, watchin' his face like hawks while they jawed an' jabbered about the cuteness an' brillance of th' no-neck monsters!

She giggles with a hand fluttering at her throat and her breast and her long throat arched.

She comes downstage and recreates the scene with voice and gesture.

And the no-neck monsters were ranged around the table, some in high chairs and some on th' *Books of Knowledge*, all in fancy little paper caps in honor of Big Daddy's birthday, and all through dinner, well, I want you to know that Brother Man an' his partner never once, for one moment, stopped exchanging pokes an' pinches an' kicks an' signs an' signals! – Why, they were like a couple of cardsharps fleecing a sucker. – Even Big Mama, bless her ole sweet soul, she isn't th' quickest an' brightest thing in the world, she finally noticed, at last, an' said to Gooper, 'Gooper, what are you an' Mae makin' all these signs at each other about?' – I swear t' goodness, I nearly choked on my chicken!

Margaret, *back at the dressing table, still doesn't see* **Brick**. *He is watching her with a look that is not quite definable – amused? shocked? contemptuous? – part of those and part of something else.*

Y'know – your brother Gooper still cherishes the illusion he took a giant step up on the social ladder when he married Miss Mae Flynn of the Memphis Flynns.

But I have a piece of Spanish news for Gooper. The Flynns never had a thing in this world but money and they lost that, they were nothing at all but fairly successful climbers. Of course, Mae Flynn came out in Memphis eight years before I made my debut in Nashville, but I had friends at Ward-Belmont who came from Memphis and they used to come to see me and I used to go to see them for Christmas and spring vacations, and so I know who rates an' who doesn't rate in Memphis society. Why, y'know ole Papa Flynn, he barely escaped doing time in the Federal pen for shady manipulations on th' stock market when his chain stores crashed, and as for Mae having been a cotton carnival queen, as they remind us so often, lest we forget, well, that's one honor that I don't envy her for! – Sit on a brass throne on a tacky float an' ride down Main Street, smilin', bowin', and blowin' kisses to all the trash on the street –

She picks out a pair of jeweled sandals and rushes to the dressing table.

Why, year before last, when Susan McPheeters was singled out fo' that honor, y' know what happened to her? Y'know what happened to poor little Susie McPheeters?

Brick (*absently*)   No. What happened to little Susie McPheeters?

Margaret   Somebody spit tobacco juice in her face.

Brick (*dreamily*)   Somebody spit tobacco juice in her face?

Margaret   That's right, some old drunk leaned out of a window in the Hotel Gayoso and yelled, 'Hey, Queen, hey, hey, there, Queenie!' Poor Susie looked up and flashed him a radiant smile and he shot out a squirt of tobacco juice right in poor Susie's face.

Brick   Well, what d'you know about that.

Margaret (*gaily*)   What do I know about it? I was there, I saw it!

Brick (*absently*)   Must have been kind of funny.

Margaret   Susie didn't think so. Had hysterics. Screamed like a banshee. They had to stop th' parade an' remove her from her throne an' go on with –

She catches sight of him in the mirror, gasps slightly, wheels about to face him. Count ten.

– Why are you looking at me like that?

Brick (*whistling softly, now*)   Like what, Maggie?

Margaret (*intensely, fearfully*)   The way y' were lookin' at me just now, befo' I caught your eye in the mirror and you started t' whistle! I don't know how t' describe it but it froze my blood! – I've caught you lookin' at me like that so often lately. What are you thinkin' of when you look at me like that?

Brick   I wasn't conscious of lookin' at you, Maggie.

Margaret   Well, I was conscious of it! What were you thinkin'?

Brick   I don't remember thinking of anything, Maggie.

Margaret   Don't you think I know that – ? Don't you – ? – Think I know that – ?

Brick (*coolly*)   Know *what*, Maggie?

Margaret (*struggling for expression*)   That I've gone through this – *hideous!* – *transformation*, become – *hard! Frantic!*

Then she adds, almost tenderly:

– *cruel!!*

That's what you've been observing in me lately. How could y' help but observe it? That's all right. I'm not – thin-skinned any more, can't afford t' be thin-skinned any more.

She is now recovering her power.

– But Brick? Brick?

Brick   Did you say something?

Margaret   I was *goin'* t' say something: that I get – lonely.
Very!

Brick   Ev'rybody gets that . . .

Margaret   Living with someone you love can be lonelier –
than living entirely *alone*! – if the one that y' love doesn't love
you . . .

There is a pause. **Brick** *hobbles downstage and asks, without looking at
her:*

Brick   Would you like to live alone, Maggie?

Another pause: then – after she has caught a quick, hurt breath:

Margaret   *No! – God! – I wouldn't!*

*Another gasping breath. She forcibly controls what must have been an
impulse to cry out. We see her deliberately, very forcibly, going all the way
back to the world in which you can talk about ordinary matters.*

Did you have a nice shower?

Brick   Uh-huh.

Margaret   Was the water cool?

Brick   No.

Margaret   But it made y' feel fresh, huh?

Brick   Fresher . . .

Margaret   I know something would make y' feel *much*
fresher!

Brick   What?

Margaret   An alcohol rub. Or cologne, a rub with cologne!

Brick   That's good after a workout but I haven't been
workin' out, Maggie.

Margaret   You've kept in good shape, though.

Brick (*indifferently*)   You think so, Maggie?

Margaret   I always thought drinkin' men lost their looks, but I was plainly mistaken.

Brick (*wryly*)   Why, thanks, Maggie.

Margaret   You're the only drinkin' man I know that it never seems t' put fat on.

Brick   I'm gettin' softer, Maggie.

Margaret   Well, sooner or later it's bound to soften you up. It was just beginning to soften up Skipper when –

She stops short.

I'm sorry. I never could keep my fingers off a sore – I wish you *would* lose your looks. If you did it would make the martyrdom of Saint Maggie a little more bearable. But no such goddam luck. I actually believe you've gotten better looking since you've gone on the bottle. Yeah, a person who didn't know you would think you'd never had a tense nerve in your body or a strained muscle.

There are sounds of croquet on the lawn below: the click of mallets, light voices, near and distant.

Of course, you always had that detached quality as if you were playing a game without much concern over whether you won or lost, and now that you've lost the game, not lost but just quit playing, you have that rare sort of charm that usually only happens in very old or hopelessly sick people, the charm of the defeated. – You look so cool, so cool, so enviably cool.

Reverend Tooker (*off stage right*)   Now looka here, boy, lemme show you how to get outa that!

Margaret   They're playing croquet. The moon has appeared and it's white, just beginning to turn a little bit yellow . . .

You were a wonderful lover . . .

Such a wonderful person to go to bed with, and I think mostly because you were really indifferent to it. Isn't that right? Never had any anxiety about it, did it naturally, easily, slowly, with absolute confidence and perfect calm, more like opening a door for a lady or seating her at a table than giving expression to any longing for her. Your indifference made you wonderful at lovemaking – *strange*? – but true . . .

Reverend Tooker   Oh! That's a beauty.

Doctor Baugh   Yeah. I got you boxed.

Margaret   You know, if I thought you would never, never, *never* make love to me again – I would go downstairs to the kitchen and pick out the longest and sharpest knife I could find and stick it straight into my heart, I swear that I would!

Reverend Tooker   Watch out, you're gonna miss it.

Doctor Baugh   You just don't know me, boy!

Margaret   But one thing I don't have is the charm of the defeated, my hat is still in the ring, and I am determined to win!

There is the sound of croquet mallets hitting croquet balls.

Reverend Tooker   Mmm – You're too slippery for me.

Margaret   – What is the victory of a cat on a hot tin roof? – I wish I knew . . .

Just staying on it, I guess, as long as she can . . .

Doctor Baugh   Jus' like an eel, boy, jus' like an eel!

More croquet sounds.

Margaret   Later tonight I'm going to tell you I love you an' maybe by that time you'll be drunk enough to believe me. Yes, they're playing croquet . . .

Big Daddy is dying of cancer . . .

What were you thinking of when I caught you looking at me like that? Were you thinking of Skipper?

Brick *takes up his crutch, rises.*

Margaret   Oh, excuse me, forgive me, but laws of silence don't work! No, laws of silence don't work . . .

Brick *crosses to the bar, takes a quick drink, and rubs his head with a towel.*

Margaret   Laws of silence don't work . . .

When something is festering in your memory or your imagination, laws of silence don't work, it's just like shutting a door and locking it on a house on fire in hope of forgetting that the house is burning. But not facing a fire doesn't put it out. Silence about a thing just magnifies it. It grows and festers in silence, becomes malignant . . .

He drops his crutch.

Brick   Give me my crutch.

He has stopped rubbing his hair dry but still stands hanging onto the towel rack in a white towel-cloth robe.

Margaret   Lean on me.

Brick   No, just give me my crutch.

Margaret   Lean on my shoulder.

Brick   *I don't want to lean on your shoulder, I want my crutch!*

This is spoken like sudden lightning.

Are you going to give me my crutch or do I have to get down on my knees on the floor and –

Margaret   *Here, here, take it, take it!*

She has thrust the crutch at him.

Brick (*hobbling out*)   Thanks . . .

Margaret   We mustn't scream at each other, the walls in this house have ears . . .

He hobbles directly to liquor cabinet to get a new drink.

– but that's the first time I've heard you raise your voice in a long time, Brick. A crack in the wall? – of composure?

– I think that's a good sign . . .

A sign of nerves in a player on the defensive!

Brick *turns and smiles at her coolly over his fresh drink.*

Brick   It just hasn't happened yet, Maggie.

Margaret   What?

Brick   The click I get in my head when I've had enough of this stuff to make me peaceful . . .

Will you do me a favor?

Margaret   Maybe I will. What favor?

Brick   Just, just keep your voice down!

Margaret (*in a hoarse whisper*)   I'll do you that favor, I'll speak in a whisper, if not shut up completely, if *you* will do *me* a favor and make that drink your last one till after the party.

Brick   What party?

Margaret   Big Daddy's birthday party.

Brick   Is this Big Daddy's birthday?

Margaret   You know this is Big Daddy's birthday!

Brick   No, I don't, I forgot it.

Margaret   Well, I remembered it for you . . .

They are both speaking as breathlessly as a pair of kids after a fight, drawing deep exhausted breaths and looking at each other with faraway eyes, shaking and panting together as if they had broken apart from a violent struggle.

Brick   Good for you, Maggie.

Margaret   You just have to scribble a few lines on this card.

Brick   You scribble something, Maggie.

Margaret   It's got to be your handwriting; it's your present, I've given him my present; it's got to be your handwriting!

The tension between them is building again, the voices becoming shrill once more.

Brick   I didn't get him a present.

Margaret   I got one for you.

Brick   All right. You write the card, then.

Margaret   And have him know you didn't remember his birthday?

Brick   I didn't remember his birthday.

Margaret   You don't have to prove you didn't!

Brick   I don't want to fool him about it.

Margaret   Just write 'Love, Brick!' for God's –

Brick   No.

Margaret   You've *got* to!

Brick   I don't have to do anything I don't want to do. You keep forgetting the conditions on which I agreed to stay on living with you.

Margaret (*out before she knows it*)   I'm not living with you. We occupy the same cage.

Brick   You've got to remember the conditions agreed on.

Sonny (*off stage*)   Mommy, give it to me. I had it first.

Mae   Hush.

Margaret   They're impossible conditions!

Brick   Then why don't you – ?

Sonny   I want it, I want it!

Mae   Getaway!

Margaret   HUSH! Who is out there? Is somebody at the door?

There are footsteps in hall.

Mae (*outside*)   May I enter a moment?

Margaret   Oh, *you*! Sure. Come in, Mae.

Mae *enters bearing aloft the bow of a young lady's archery set.*

Mae   Brick, is this thing yours?

Margaret   Why, Sister Woman – that's my Diana Trophy. Won it at the intercollegiate archery contest on the Ole Miss campus.

Mae   It's a mighty dangerous thing to leave exposed round a house full of nawmal rid-blooded children attracted t'weapons.

Margaret   'Nawmal rid-blooded children attracted t'weapons' ought t'be taught to keep their hands off things that don't belong to them.

Mae   Maggie, honey, if you had children of your own you'd know how funny that is. Will you please lock this up and put the key out of reach?

Margaret   Sister Woman, nobody is plotting the destruction of your kiddies. – Brick and I still have our special archers' license. We're goin' deer-huntin' on Moon Lake as soon as the season starts. I love to run with dogs through chilly woods, run, run, leap over obstructions –

She goes into the closet carrying the bow.

Mae   How's the injured ankle, Brick?

Brick   Doesn't hurt. Just itches.

Mae   Oh, my! Brick – Brick, you should've been downstairs after supper! Kiddies put on a show. Polly played the piano, Buster an' Sonny drums, an' then they turned out the lights an' Dixie an' Trixie puhfawmed a toe dance in fairy costume with *spahkluhs*! Big Daddy just beamed! He just beamed!

Margaret (*from the closet with a sharp laugh*)   Oh, I bet. It breaks my heart that we missed it!

She re-enters.

But Mae? Why did y'give dawgs' names to all your kiddies?

Mae   *Dogs'* names?

Margaret (*sweetly*)   Dixie, Trixie, Buster, Sonny, Polly! – Sounds like four dogs and a parrot . . .

Mae   Maggie?

Margaret *turns with a smile.*

Mae   Why are you so catty?

Margaret   'Cause I'm a cat! But why can't *you* take a joke, Sister Woman?

Mae   Nothin' pleases me more than a joke that's funny. You know the real names of our kiddies. Buster's real name is Robert. Sonny's real name is Saunders. Trixie's real name is Marlene and Dixie's –

Gooper *downstairs calls for her.* '*Hey, Mae! Sister Woman, intermission is over!*' – *She rushes to door, saying:*

Mae   Intermission is over! See ya later!

Margaret   I wonder what Dixie's real name is?

Brick   Maggie, being catty doesn't help things any . . .

Margaret   I know! *WHY!* – Am I so catty? – 'Cause I'm consumed with envy an' eaten up with longing? – Brick, I'm going to lay out your beautiful Shantung silk suit from Rome and one of your monogrammed silk shirts. I'll put your cuff links in it, those lovely star sapphires I get you to wear so rarely . . .

Brick   I can't get trousers on over this plaster cast.

Margaret   Yes, you can, I'll help you.

Brick   I'm not going to get dressed, Maggie.

Margaret   Will you just put on a pair of white silk pajamas?

Brick   Yes, I'll do that, Maggie.

Margaret   *Thank* you, thank you so *much*!

Brick   Don't mention it.

Margaret   *Oh, Brick*! How long does it have t' go on? This punishment? Haven't I done time enough, haven't I served my term, can't I apply for a – pardon?

Brick   Maggie, you're spoiling my liquor. Lately your voice always sounds like you'd been running upstairs to warn somebody that the house was on fire!

Margaret   Well, no wonder, no wonder. Y'know what I feel like, Brick?

I feel all the time like a cat on a hot tin roof!

Brick   Then jump off the roof, jump off it, cats can jump off roofs and land on their four feet uninjured!

Margaret   Oh, yes!

Brick   Do it! – fo' God's sake, do it . . .

Margaret   Do what?

Brick   Take a lover!

Margaret   I can't see a man but you! Even with my eyes closed, I just see you! Why don't you get ugly, Brick, why don't you please get fat or ugly or something so I could stand it?

She rushes to hall door, opens it, listens.

The concert is still going on! Bravo, no-necks, bravo! (*She slams and locks door fiercely.*)

Brick   What did you lock the door for?

Margaret   To give us a little privacy for a while.

Brick   You know better, Maggie.

Margaret   No, I don't know better . . .

She rushes to gallery doors, draws the rose-silk drapes across them.

Brick   Don't make a fool of yourself.

Margaret   I don't mind makin' a fool of myself over you!

Brick   I mind, Maggie. I feel embarrassed for you.

Margaret   Feel embarrassed! But don't continue my torture. I can't live on and on under these circumstances.

Brick   You agreed to –

Margaret   I know but –

Brick   – Accept that condition!

Margaret   *I CAN'T! CAN'T! CAN'T!*

She seizes his shoulder.

Brick   Let go!

He breaks away from her and seizes the small boudoir chair and raises it like a lion-tamer facing a big circus cat.

Count five. She stares at him with her fist pressed to her mouth, then bursts into shrill, almost hysterical laughter. He remains grave for a moment, then grins and puts the chair down.

Big Mama *calls through closed door.*

Big Mama   Son? Son? Son?

Brick   What is it, Big Mama?

Big Mama (*outside*)   Oh, son! We got the most wonderful news about Big Daddy. I just had t' run up an' tell you right this –

She rattles the knob.

– What's this door doin', locked, faw? You all think there's robbers in the house?

Margaret   Big Mama, Brick is dressin', he's not dressed yet.

Big Mama   That's all right, it won't be the first time I've seen Brick not dressed. Come on, open this door!

Margaret, *with a grimace, goes to unlock and open the hall door, as* **Brick** *hobbles rapidly to the bathroom and kicks the door shut.* **Big Mama** *has disappeared from the hall.*

Margaret   Big Mama?

Big Mama *appears through the opposite gallery doors behind* **Margaret**, *huffing and puffing like an old bulldog. She is a short, stout woman; her sixty years and 170 pounds have left her somewhat breathless most of the time; she's always tensed like a boxer, or rather, a Japanese wrestler. Her 'family' was maybe a little superior to* **Big Daddy**'*s, but not much. She wears a black or silver lace dress and at least half a million in flashy gems. She is very sincere.*

Big Mama (*loudly, startling* **Margaret**)   Here – I come through Gooper's and Mae's gall'ry door. Where's Brick? *Brick* – Hurry on out of there, son, I just have a second and want to give you the news about Big Daddy. I hate locked doors in a house . . .

Margaret (*with affected lightness*)   I've noticed you do, Big Mama, but people have got to have *some* moments of privacy, don't they?

Big Mama   No, ma'am, not in *my* house. (*Without pause.*) Whacha took off you' dress faw? I thought that little lace dress was so sweet on yuh, honey.

Margaret   I thought it looked sweet on me, too, but one of m' cute little table-partners used it for a napkin so – !

Big Mama (*picking up stockings on floor*)   What?

Margaret   You know, Big Mama, Mae and Gooper's so touchy about those children – thanks, Big Mama . . .

Big Mama *has thrust the picked-up stockings in* **Margaret**'*s hand with a grunt.*

Margaret   – that you just don't dare to suggest there's any room for improvement in their –

Big Mama   Brick, hurry out! – Shoot, Maggie, you just don't like children.

Margaret   I do SO like children! Adore them! – well brought up!

Big Mama (*gentle-loving*)   Well, why don't you have some and bring them up well, then, instead of all the time pickin' on Gooper's an' Mae's?

Gooper (*shouting up the stairs*)   Hey, hey, Big Mama, Betsy an' Hugh got to go, waitin' t' tell yuh g'by!

Big Mama   Tell 'em to hold their hawses, I'll be right down in a jiffy!

Gooper   Yes ma'am!

She turns to the bathroom door and calls out.

Big Mama   Son? Can you hear me in there?

There is a muffled answer.

We just got the full report from the laboratory at the Ochsner Clinic, completely negative, son, ev'rything negative, right on down the line! Nothin' a-tall's wrong with him but some little functional thing called a spastic colon. Can you hear me, son?

Margaret   He can hear you, Big Mama.

Big Mama   Then why don't he say something? God Almighty, a piece of news like that should make him shout. It made *me* shout, I can tell you. I shouted and sobbed and fell right down on my knees! – Look!

She pulls up her skirt.

See the bruises where I hit my kneecaps? Took both doctors to haul me back on my feet!

She laughs – she always laughs like hell at herself.

Big Daddy was furious with me! But ain't that wonderful news?

Pacing bathroom again, she continues:

After all the anxiety we been through to git a report like that on Big Daddy's birthday? Big Daddy tried to hide how much of a load that news took off his mind, but didn't fool *me*. He was mighty close to crying about it *himself*!

Goodbyes are shouted downstairs, and she rushes to door.

Gooper   Big Mama!

Big Mama   *Hold those people down there, don't let them go!* – Now, git dressed, we're all comin' up to this room fo' Big Daddy's birthday party because of your ankle. – How's his ankle, Maggie?

Margaret   Well, he broke it, Big Mama.

Big Mama   I know he broke it.

A phone is ringing in hall. A Negro voice answers: 'Mistuh Polly's res'dence.'

I mean does it hurt him much still.

Margaret   I'm afraid I can't give you that information, Big Mama. You'll have to ask Brick if it hurts much still or not.

Sookey (*in the hall*)   It's Memphis, Mizz Polly, it's Miss Sally in Memphis.

Big Mama   Awright, Sookey.

She rushes into the hall and is heard shouting on the phone:

Hello, Miss Sally. How are you, Miss Sally? – Yes, well, I was just gonna call you about it. *Shoot!* –

Margaret   Brick, don't!

Big Mama *raises her voice to a bellow.*

Big Mama   *Miss Sally? Don't ever call me from the Gayoso Lobby, too much talk goes on in that hotel lobby, no wonder you can't hear me!* Now listen, Miss Sally. They's nothin' serious wrong with Big Daddy. We got the report just now, they's nothin' wrong but a thing called a – spastic! *SPASTIC!* – colon . . .

*She appears at the hall door and calls to **Margaret**.*

Big Mama   − Maggie, come out here and talk to that fool on the phone. I'm shouted breathless!

Margaret (*goes out and is heard sweetly at phone*)   Miss Sally? This is Brick's wife, Maggie. So nice to hear your voice. Can you hear *mine*? Well, *good*! Big Mama just wanted you to know that they've got the report from the Ochsner Clinic and what Big Daddy has is a spastic colon. Yes. Spastic colon, Miss Sally. That's right, spastic colon. *G'bye, Miss Sally, hope I'll see you real soon!*

Hangs up a little before Miss Sally was probably ready to terminate the talk. She returns through the hall door.

She heard me perfectly. I've discovered with deaf people the thing to do is not shout at them but just enunciate clearly. My rich old Aunt Cornelia was deaf as the dead but I could make her hear me just by sayin' each word slowly, distinctly, close to her ear. I read her the *Commercial Appeal* ev'ry night, read her the classified ads in it, even, she never missed a word of it. But was she a mean ole thing! Know what I got when she died? Her unexpired subscriptions to five magazines and the Book-of-the-Month Club and a LIBRARY full of ev'ry dull book ever written! All else went to her hellcat of a sister . . . meaner than she was, even!

Big Mama *has been straightening things up in the room during this speech.*

Big Mama (*closing closet door on discarded clothes*)   *Miss Sally sure is a case!* Big Daddy says she's always got her hand out fo' something. He's not mistaken. That poor ole thing always has her hand out fo' somethin'. I don't think Big Daddy gives her as much as he should.

Gooper   Big Mama! Come on now! Betsy and Hugh can't wait no longer!

Big Mama (*shouting*)   I'm comin'!

She starts out. At the hall door, turns and jerks a forefinger, first toward the bathroom door, then toward the liquor cabinet, meaning: 'Has Brick been drinking?' **Margaret** *pretends not to understand, cocks her head* *and raises her brows as if the pantomimic performance was completely mystifying to her.*

Big Mama *rushes back to* **Margaret***:*

Big Mama   *Shoot! Stop playin' so dumb!* – I mean has he been drinkin' that stuff much yet?

Margaret (*with a little laugh*)   Oh! I think he had a highball after supper.

Big Mama   Don't laugh about it! – Some single men stop drinkin' when they git married and others start! Brick never touched liquor before he – !

Margaret (*crying out*)   *THAT'S NOT FAIR!*

Big Mama   Fair or not fair I want to ask you a question, one question: D'you make Brick happy in bed?

Margaret   Why don't you ask if he makes *me* happy in bed?

Big Mama   Because I know that –

Margaret   *It works both ways!*

Big Mama   Something's not right! You're childless and my son drinks!

Gooper   Come on, Big Mama!

Gooper *has called her downstairs and she has rushed to the door on the line above. She turns at the door and points at the bed.*

Big Mama   – When a marriage goes on the rocks, the rocks are *there*, right *there*!

Margaret   *That's* –

Big Mama *has swept out of the room and slammed the door.*

Margaret   – not – *fair* . . .

Margaret *is alone, completely alone, and she feels it. She draws in, hunches her shoulders, raises her arms with fists clenched, shuts her eyes tight as a child about to be stabbed with a vaccination needle. When she opens her eyes again, what she sees is the long oval mirror and she rushes*

*straight to it, stares into it with a grimace and says: 'Who are you?' –
Then she crouches a little and answers herself in a different voice which
is high, thin, mocking: 'I am Maggie the Cat!' – Straightens quickly as
bathroom door opens a little and* **Brick** *calls out to her.*

Brick   Has Big Mama gone?

Margaret   She's gone.

*He opens the bathroom door and hobbles out, with his liquor glass now
empty, straight to the liquor cabinet. He is whistling softly.* **Margaret**'s
head pivots on her long, slender throat to watch him.

*She raises a hand uncertainly to the base of her throat, as if it was
difficult for her to swallow, before she speaks:*

You know, our sex life didn't just peter out in the usual way, it
was cut off short, long before the natural time for it to, and it's
going to revive again, just as sudden as that. I'm confident of it.
That's what I'm keeping myself attractive for. For the time
when you'll see me again like other men see me. Yes, like other
men see me. They still see me, Brick, and they like what they
see. Uh-huh. Some of them would give their –

Look, Brick!

*She stands before the long oval mirror, touches her breast and then her
hips with her two hands.*

How high my body stays on me! – Nothing has fallen on me –
not a fraction . . .

*Her voice is soft and trembling: a pleading child's. At this moment as he
turns to glance at her – a look which is like a player passing a ball to
another player, third down and goal to go – she has to capture the
audience in a grip so tight that she can hold it till the first intermission
without any lapse of attention.*

Other men still want me. My face looks strained, sometimes,
but I've kept my figure as well as you've kept yours, and men
admire it. I still turn heads on the street. Why, last week in
Memphis everywhere that I went men's eyes burned holes in my
clothes, at the country club and in restaurants and department
stores, there wasn't a man I met or walked by that didn't just

eat me up with his eyes and turn around when I passed him
and look back at me. Why, at Alice's party for her New York
cousins, the best-lookin' man in the crowd – followed me
upstairs and tried to force his way in the powder room with
me, followed me to the door and tried to force his way in.

Brick Why didn't you let him, Maggie?

Margaret Because I'm not that common, for one thing. Not
that I wasn't almost tempted to. You like to know who it was?
It was Sonny Boy Maxwell, that's who!

Brick Oh, yeah, Sonny Boy Maxwell, he was a good end-
runner but had a little injury to his back and had to quit.

Margaret He has no injury now and has no wife and still
has a lech for me!

Brick I see no reason to lock him out of a powder room in
that case.

Margaret And have someone catch me at it? I'm not that
stupid. Oh, I might sometime cheat on you with someone,
since you're so insultingly eager to have me do it! – But if I do,
you can be damned sure it will be in a place and a time where
no one but me and the man could possibly know. Because I'm
not going to give you any excuse to divorce me for being
unfaithful or anything else . . .

Brick Maggie, I wouldn't divorce you for being unfaithful
or anything else. Don't you know that? Hell. I'd be relieved to
know that you'd found yourself a lover.

Margaret Well, I'm taking no chances. No, I'd rather stay
on this hot tin roof.

Brick A hot tin roof's 'n uncomfo'table place t' stay on . . .

He starts to whistle softly.

Margaret (*through his whistle*) Yeah, but I can stay on it just
as long as I have to.

Brick You could leave me, Maggie.

He resumes whistle. She wheels about to glare at him.

Margaret   *Don't want to and will not!* Besides if I did, you don't have a cent to pay for it but what you get from Big Daddy and he's dying of cancer!

*For the first time a realization of **Big Daddy**'s doom seems to penetrate to **Brick**'s consciousness, visibly, and he looks at **Margaret**.*

Brick   Big Mama just said he *wasn't*, that the report was okay.

Margaret   That's what she thinks because she got the same story that they gave Big Daddy. And was just as taken in by it as he was, poor ole things . . .

But tonight they're going to tell her the truth about it. When Big Daddy goes to bed, they're going to tell her that he is dying of cancer.

She slams the dresser drawer.

– It's malignant and it's terminal.

Brick   Does Big Daddy know it?

Margaret   Hell, do they *ever* know it? Nobody says, 'You're dying.' You have to fool them. They have to fool *themselves*.

Brick   Why?

Margaret   *Why?* Because human beings dream of life everlasting, that's the reason! But most of them want it on earth and not in heaven.

He gives a short, hard laugh at her touch of humor.

Well . . . (*She touches up her mascara.*) That's how it is, anyhow . . . (*She looks about.*) Where did I put down my cigarette? Don't want to burn up the home-place, at least not with Mae and Gooper and their five monsters in it!

She has found it and sucks at it greedily. Blows out smoke and continues:

So this is Big Daddy's last birthday. And Mae and Gooper, they know it, oh, *they* know it, all right. They got the first

information from the Ochsner Clinic. That's why they rushed
down here with their no-neck monsters. Because. Do you know
something? Big Daddy's made no will? Big Daddy's never
made out any will in his life, and so this campaign's afoot to
impress him, forcibly as possible, with the fact that you drink
and I've borne no children!

*He continues to stare at her a moment, then mutters something sharp but
not audible and hobbles rather rapidly out onto the long gallery in the
fading, much faded, gold light.*

Margaret (*continuing her liturgical chant*) Y'know, I'm *fond* of
Big Daddy, I am genuinely fond of that old man, I really *am*,
you know . . .

Brick (*faintly, vaguely*) Yes, I know you are . . .

Margaret I've always sort of admired him in spite of his
coarseness, his four-letter words and so forth. Because Big
Daddy *is* what he *is*, and he makes no bones about it. He
hasn't turned gentleman farmer, he's still a Mississippi redneck,
as much of a redneck as he must have been when he was just
overseer here on the old Jack Straw and Peter Ochello place.
But he got hold of it an' built it into th' biggest an' finest
plantation in the Delta. – I've always *liked* Big Daddy . . .

She crosses to the proscenium.

Well, this is Big Daddy's last birthday. I'm sorry about it. But
I'm facing the facts. It takes money to take care of a drinker
and that's the office that I've been elected to lately.

Brick You don't have to take care of me.

Margaret Yes, I do. Two people in the same boat have got
to take care of each other. At least you want money to buy
more Echo Spring when this supply is exhausted, or will you
be satisfied with a ten-cent beer?

Mae an' Gooper are plannin' to freeze us out of Big Daddy's
estate because you drink and I'm childless. But we can defeat
that plan. We're *going* to defeat that plan!

Brick, y'know, I've been so God damn disgustingly poor all my life! –
That's the *truth*, Brick!

Brick   I'm not sayin' it isn't.

Margaret   Always had to suck up to people I couldn't stand
because they had money and I was poor as Job's turkey. You
don't know what that's like. Well, I'll tell you, it's like you
would feel a thousand miles away from Echo Spring! – And
had to get back to it on that broken ankle . . . without a crutch!

That's how it feels to be as poor as Job's turkey and have to
suck up to relatives that you hated because they had money
and all you had was a bunch of hand-me-down clothes and a
few old moldly three-per-cent government bonds. My daddy
loved his liquor, he fell in love with his liquor the way you've
fallen in love with Echo Spring! – And my poor Mama, having
to maintain some semblance of social position, to keep
appearances up, on an income of one hundred and fifty dollars
a month on those old government bonds!

When I came out, the year that I made my debut, I had just
two evening dresses! One Mother made me from a pattern in
Vogue, the other a hand-me-down from a snotty rich cousin
I hated!

– The dress that I married you in was my grandmother's
weddin' gown . . .

So that's why I'm like a cat on a hot tin roof!

Brick *is still on the gallery. Someone below calls up to him in a warm
Negro voice, 'Hiya, Mistuh Brick, how yuh feelin'?'* **Brick** *raises his
liquor glass as if that answered the question.*

Margaret   You can be young without money, but you can't
be old without it. You've got to be old *with* money because to
be old without it is just too awful, you've got to be one or the
other, either *young* or *with money*, you can't be old and *without* it.
– That's the *truth*, Brick . . .

Brick *whistles softly, vaguely.*

Margaret   Well, now I'm dressed, I'm all dressed, there's nothing else for me to do.

Forlornly, almost fearfully.

I'm dressed, all dressed, nothing else for me to do . . .

She moves about restlessly, aimlessly, and speaks, as if to herself.

What am I – ? Oh! – my bracelets . . .

She starts working a collection of bracelets over her hands onto her wrists, about six on each, as she talks.

I've thought a whole lot about it and now I know when I made my mistake. Yes, I made my mistake when I told you the truth about that thing with Skipper. Never should have confessed it, a fatal error, tellin' you about that thing with Skipper.

Brick   Maggie, shut up about Skipper. I mean it, Maggie; you got to shut up about Skipper.

Margaret   You ought to understand that Skipper and I –

Brick   You don't think I'm serious, Maggie? You're fooled by the fact that I am saying this quiet? Look, Maggie. What you're doing is a dangerous thing to do. You're – you're – you're – foolin' with something that – nobody ought to fool with.

Margaret   This time I'm going to finish what I have to say to you. Skipper and I made love, if love you could call it, because it made both of us feel a little bit closer to you. You see, you son of a bitch, you asked too much of people, of me, of him, of all the unlucky poor damned sons of bitches that happen to love you, and there was a whole pack of them, yes, there was a pack of them besides me and Skipper, you asked too goddam much of people that loved you, you – superior creature! – you godlike being! – And so we made love to each other to dream it was you, both of us! Yes, yes, yes! Truth, truth! What's so awful about it? I like it, I think the truth is – yeah! I shouldn't have told you . . .

Brick (*holding his head unnaturally still and uptilted a bit*)   It was Skipper that told me about it. Not you, Maggie.

Margaret   I told you!

Brick   After he told me!

Margaret   What does it matter who – ?

Dixie   I got your mallet, I got your mallet.

Trixie   Give it to me, give it to me. It's mine.

Brick *turns suddenly out upon the gallery and calls:*

Brick   Little girl! Hey, little girl!

Little Girl (*at a distance*)   What, Uncle Brick?

Brick   Tell the folks to come up! – Bring everybody upstairs!

Trixie   It's mine, it's mine.

Margaret   I can't stop myself! I'd go on telling you this in front of them all, if I had to!

Brick   Little girl! Go on, go on, will you? Do what I told you, call them!

Dixie   Okay.

Margaret   Because it's got to be told and you, you! – you never let me!

She sobs, then controls herself, and continues almost calmly.

It was one of those beautiful, ideal things they tell about in the Greek legends, it couldn't be anything else, you being you, and that's what made it so sad, that's what made it so awful, because it was love that never could be carried through to anything satisfying or even talked about plainly.

Brick   Maggie, you gotta stop this.

Margaret   Brick, I tell you, you got to believe me, Brick, I *do* understand all about it! I – I think it was – *noble*! Can't you tell I'm sincere when I say I respect it? My only point, the only point that I'm making, is life has got to be allowed to continue even after the *dream* of life is – all – over . . .

Brick *is without his crutch. Leaning on furniture, he crosses to pick it up as she continues as if possessed by a will outside herself:*

Margaret   Why I remember when we double-dated at college, Gladys Fitzgerald and I and you and Skipper, it was more like a date between you and Skipper. Gladys and I were just sort of tagging along as – if it was necessary to chaperone you! – to make a good public impression –

Brick (*turns to face her, half lifting his crutch*)   Maggie, you want me to hit you with this crutch? Don't you know I could kill you with this crutch?

Margaret   Good Lord, man, d' you think I'd care if you did?

Brick   One man has one great good true thing in his life. One great good thing which is true! – I had friendship with Skipper. – You are naming it dirty!

Margaret   I'm not naming it dirty! I am naming it clean.

Brick   Not love with you, Maggie, but friendship with Skipper was that one great true thing, and you are naming it dirty!

Margaret   Then you haven't been listenin', not understood what I'm saying! I'm naming it so damn clean that it killed poor Skipper! – You two had something that had to be kept on ice, yes, incorruptible, yes! – and death was the only icebox where you could keep it . . .

Brick   I married you, Maggie. Why would I marry you, Maggie, if I was – ?

Margaret   Brick, let me finish! – I know, believe me I know, that it was only Skipper that harbored even any *unconscious* desire for anything not perfectly pure between you two! – Now let me skip a little. You married me early that summer we graduated out of Ole Miss, and we were happy, weren't we, we were blissful, yes, hit heaven together ev'ry time that we loved! But that fall you an' Skipper turned down wonderful offers of jobs in order to keep on bein' football heroes – pro-football heroes. You organized the Dixie Stars that fall, so you could keep on bein' teammates forever! But somethin' was not right with it! – *Me included!* – between you. Skipper began hittin' the bottle . . . you got a spinal injury – couldn't play the Thanksgivin' game in Chicago, watched it on TV from a traction bed in Toledo. I joined Skipper. The Dixie Stars lost because poor Skipper was drunk. We drank together that night all night in the bar of the Blackstone and when cold day was comin' up over the Lake an' we were comin' out drunk to take a dizzy look at it, I said, 'SKIPPER! STOP LOVIN' MY HUSBAND OR TELL HIM HE'S GOT TO LET YOU ADMIT IT TO HIM!' – one way or another!

HE SLAPPED ME HARD ON THE MOUTH! – then turned and ran without stopping once, I am sure, all the way back into his room at the Blackstone . . .

– When I came to his room that night, with a little scratch like a shy little mouse at his door, he made that pitiful, ineffectual little attempt to prove that what I had said wasn't true . . .

Brick *strikes at her with crutch, a blow that shatters the gemlike lamp on the table.*

Margaret   – In this way, I destroyed him, by telling him truth that he and his world which he was born and raised in, yours and his world, had told him could not be told?

– From then on Skipper was nothing at all but a receptacle for liquor and drugs . . .

– *Who shot cock robin? I with my –*

She throws back her head with tight shut eyes.

– *merciful arrow!*

Brick *strikes at her; misses.*

Margaret   Missed me! – Sorry – I'm not tryin' to whitewash my behavior, Christ, no! Brick, I'm not good. I don't know why people have to pretend to be good, nobody's good. The rich or the well-to-do can afford to respect moral patterns, conventional moral patterns, but I could never afford to, yeah, but –

I'm honest! Give me credit for just that, will you *please*? Born poor, raised poor, expect to die poor unless I manage to get us something out of what Big Daddy leaves when he dies of cancer! But Brick?! – *Skipper is dead! I'm alive!* Maggie the cat is –

Brick *hops awkwardly forward and strikes at her again with his crutch.*

Margaret   – *alive! I am alive, alive! I am . . .*

He hurls the crutch at her, across the bed she took refuge behind, and pitches forward on the floor as she completes her speech.

Margaret   – *alive!*

A little girl, **Dixie**, *bursts into the room, wearing an Indian war bonnet and firing a cap pistol at* **Margaret** *and shouting: 'Bang, bang, bang!'*

Laughter downstairs floats through the open hall door. **Margaret** *had crouched gasping to bed at child's entrance. She now rises and says with cool fury:*

Little girl, your mother or someone should teach you – (*Gasping.*) – to knock at a door before you come into a room. Otherwise people might think that you – lack – good breeding . . .

Dixie   Yanh, yanh, yanh, what is Uncle Brick doin' on th' floor?

Brick   I tried to kill your Aunt Maggie, but I failed – and I fell. Little girl, give me my crutch so I can get up off th' floor.

Margaret   Yes, give your uncle his crutch, he's a cripple, honey, he broke his ankle last night jumping hurdles on the high school athletic field!

Dixie   What were you jumping hurdles for, Uncle Brick?

Brick   Because I used to jump them, and people like to do what they used to do, even after they've stopped being able to do it . . .

Margaret   That's right, that's your answer, now go away, little girl.

Dixie *fires cap pistol at* **Margaret** *three times.*

Margaret   *Stop, you stop that, monster! You little no-neck monster!*

She seizes the cap pistol and hurls it through gallery doors.

Dixie (*with a precocious instinct for the cruelest thing*)   You're
jealous! – You're just jealous because you can't have babies!

She sticks out her tongue at **Margaret** *as she sashays past her with her
stomach stuck out, to the gallery.* **Margaret** *slams the gallery doors
and leans panting against them.*

There is a pause. **Brick** *has replaced his spilt drink and sits, faraway,
on the great four-poster bed.*

Margaret   You see? – they gloat over us being childless,
even in front of their five little no-neck monsters!

Pause. Voices approach on the stairs.

Brick? – I've been to a doctor in Memphis, a – a gynecologist . . .

I've been completely examined, and there is no reason why we
can't have a child whenever we want one. And this is my time
by the calendar to conceive. Are you listening to me? Are you?
Are you LISTENING TO ME!

Brick   Yes. I hear you, Maggie.

His attention returns to her inflamed face.

– But how in hell on earth do you imagine – that you're going
to have a child by a man that can't stand you?

Margaret   That's a problem that I will have to work out.

She wheels about to face the hall door.

Mae (*off stage left*)   Come on, Big Daddy. We're all goin' up to
Brick's room.

From off stage left, voices: **Reverend Tooker**, **Doctor Baugh**,
Mae.

Margaret   *Here they come!*

The lights dim.

Curtain.

Act Two

There is no lapse of time. **Margaret** *and* **Brick** *are in the same positions they held at the end of Act One.*

Margaret (*at door*) Here they come!

Big Daddy *appears first, a tall man with a fierce, anxious look, moving carefully not to betray his weakness even, or especially, to himself.*

Gooper I read in the *Register* that you're getting a new memorial window.

Some of the people are approaching through the hall, others along the gallery: voices from both directions. **Gooper** *and* **Reverend Tooker** *become visible outside gallery doors, and their voices come in clearly.*

They pause outside as **Gooper** *lights a cigar.*

Reverend Tooker (*vivaciously*) Oh, but St Paul's in Grenada has three memorial windows, and the latest one is a Tiffany stained-glass window that cost twenty-five hundred dollars, a picture of Christ the Good Shepherd with a Lamb in His arms.

Margaret Big Daddy.

Big Daddy Well, Brick.

Brick Hello Big Daddy. – Congratulations!

Big Daddy – Crap . . .

Gooper Who give that window, Preach?

Reverend Tooker Clyde Fletcher's widow. Also presented St Paul's with a baptismal font.

Gooper Y'know what somebody ought t' give your church is a *coolin'* system, Preach.

Mae (*almost religiously*) – Let's see now, they've had their *tyyy*-phoid shots, and their tetanus shots, their diphtheria shots and their hepatitis shots and their polio shots, they got *those* shots

every month from May through September, and – Gooper?
Hey! Gooper! What all have the kiddies been shot faw?

Reverend Tooker   Yes, siree, Bob! And y'know what Gus
Hamma's family gave in his memory to the church at Two
Rivers? A complete new stone parish-house with a basketball
court in the basement and a –

Big Daddy (*uttering a loud barking laugh which is far from truly
mirthful*)   Hey, Preach! What's all this talk about memorials,
Preach? Y' think somebody's about t' kick off around here?
'S that it?

Startled by this interjection, **Reverend Tooker** *decides to laugh at
the question almost as loud as he can.*

*How he would answer the question we'll never know, as he's spared that
embarrassment by the voice of* **Gooper**'s *wife,* **Mae**, *rising high and
clear as she appears with* **'Doc' Baugh**, *the family doctor, through the
hall door.*

Margaret (*overlapping a bit*)   Turn on the hi-fi, Brick! Let's
have some music t' start off th' party with!

Brick   You turn it on, Maggie.

*The talk becomes so general that the room sounds like a great aviary of
chattering birds. Only* **Brick** *remains unengaged, leaning upon the
liquor cabinet with his faraway smile, an ice cube in a paper napkin
with which he now and then rubs his forehead. He doesn't respond to*
Margaret's *command. She bounds forward and stoops over the
instrument panel of the console.*

Gooper   We gave 'em that thing for a third anniversary
present, got three speakers in it.

*The room is suddenly blasted by the climax of a Wagnerian opera or a
Beethoven symphony.*

Big Daddy   *Turn that dam thing off!*

Almost instant silence, almost instantly broken by the shouting charge of
Big Mama, *entering through hall door like a charging rhino.*

Big Mama   *Wha's my Brick, wha's mah precious baby!!*

Big Daddy   *Sorry! Turn it back on!*

Everyone laughs very loud. **Big Daddy** *is famous for his jokes at* **Big Mama***'s expense, and nobody laughs louder at these jokes than* **Big Mama** *herself, though sometimes they're pretty cruel and* **Big Mama** *has to pick up or fuss with something to cover the hurt that the loud laugh doesn't quite cover.*

On this occasion, a happy occasion because the dread in her heart has also been lifted by the false report on **Big Daddy***'s condition, she giggles, grotesquely, coyly, in* **Big Daddy***'s direction and bears down upon* **Brick***, all very quick and alive.*

Big Mama   Here he is, here's my precious baby! What's that you've got in your hand? You put that liquor down, son, your hand was made fo' holdin' somethin' better than that!

Gooper   Look at Brick put it down!

Brick *has obeyed* **Big Mama** *by draining the glass and handing it to her. Again everyone laughs, some high, some low.*

Big Mama   Oh, you bad boy, you, you're my bad little boy. Give Big Mama a kiss, you bad boy, you! – Look at him shy away, will you? Brick never liked bein' kissed or made a fuss over, I guess because he's always had too much of it!

Son, you turn that thing off!

Brick *has switched on the TV set.*

Big Mama   I can't stand TV, radio was bad enough but TV has gone it one better, I *mean* – (*Plops wheezing in chair.*) one worse, ha ha! Now what'm I sittin' down here faw? I want t' sit next to my sweetheart on the sofa, hold hands with him and love him up a little!

Big Mama *has on a black-and-white figured chiffon. The large irregular patterns, like the markings of some massive animal, the luster of her great diamonds and many pearls, the brilliants set in the silver frames of her glasses, her riotous voice, booming laugh, have dominated the room since she entered.* **Big Daddy** *has been regarding her with a steady grimace of chronic annoyance.*

Big Mama (*still louder*)   Preacher, Preacher, hey, Preach! Give me you' hand an' help me up from this chair!

Reverend Tooker   None of your tricks, Big Mama!

Big Mama   What tricks? You give me you' hand so I can get up an' –

Reverend Tooker *extends her his hand. She grabs it and pulls him into her lap with a shrill laugh that spans an octave in two notes.*

Big Mama   Ever seen a preacher in a fat lady's lap? Hey, hey, folks! Ever seen a preacher in a fat lady's lap?

Big Mama *is notorious throughout the Delta for this sort of inelegant horseplay.* **Margaret** *looks on with indulgent humor, sipping Dubonnet 'on the rocks' and watching* **Brick**, *but* **Mae** *and* **Gooper** *exchange signs of humorless anxiety over these antics, the sort of behavior which* **Mae** *thinks may account for their failure to quite get in with the smartest young married set in Memphis, despite all. One of the Negroes,* **Lacy** *or* **Sookey**, *peeks in, cackling. They are waiting for a sign to bring in the cake and champagne. But* **Big Daddy**'s *not amused. He doesn't understand why, in spite of the infinite mental relief he's received from the doctor's report, he still has these same old fox teeth in his guts. 'This spastic condition is something else,' he says to himself, but aloud he roars at* **Big Mama**.

Big Daddy   *BIG MAMA, WILL YOU QUIT HORSIN'?* – You're too old an' too fat fo' that sort of crazy kid stuff an' besides a woman with your blood pressure – she had two hundred last spring! – is riskin' a stroke when you mess around like that . . .

Mae *blows on a pitch pipe.*

Big Mama   *Here comes Big Daddy's birthday!*

Negroes in white jackets enter with an enormous birthday cake ablaze with candles and carrying buckets of champagne with satin ribbons about the bottle necks.

Mae *and* **Gooper** *strike up song, and everybody, including the Negroes and children, joins in. Only* **Brick** *remains aloof.*

Everyone
  Happy birthday to you.
  Happy birthday to you.
  Happy birthday, Big Daddy –

Some sing: 'Dear, Big Daddy!'

  Happy birthday to you.

Some sing: 'How old are you?'

Mae *has come down center and is organizing her children like a chorus. She gives them a barely audible: 'One, two, three!' and they are off in the new tune.*

Children
  Skinamarinka-dinka-dink
  Skinamarinka-do
  We love you.
  Skinamarinka-dinka-dink
  Skinamarinka-do.

All together, they turn to **Big Daddy**.

Children
  Big Daddy, you!

They turn back front, like a musical comedy chorus.

  We love you in the morning;
  We love you in the night.
  We love you when we're with you,
  And we love you out of sight.
  Skinamarinka-dinka-dink
  Skinamarinka-do.

Mae *turns to* **Big Mama**.

Children
  Big Mama, too!

Big Mama *bursts into tears. The Negroes leave.*

Big Daddy   Now Ida, what the hell is the matter with you?

Mae   She's just so happy.

Big Mama   I'm just so happy, Big Daddy, I have to cry or something.

Sudden and loud in the hush:

Brick, do you know the wonderful news that Doc Baugh got from the clinic about Big Daddy? Big Daddy's one hundred per cent!

Margaret   Isn't that wonderful?

Big Mama   He's just one hundred per cent. Passed the examination with flying colors. Now that we know there's nothing wrong with Big Daddy but a spastic colon, I can tell you something. I was worried sick, half out of my mind, for fear that Big Daddy might have a thing like –

Margaret *cuts through this speech, jumping up and exclaiming shrilly:*

Margaret   Brick, honey, aren't you going to give Big Daddy his birthday present?

Passing by him, she snatches his liquor glass from him. She picks up a fancily wrapped package.

Here it is, Big Daddy, this is from Brick!

Big Mama   This is the biggest birthday Big Daddy's ever had, a hundred presents and bushels of telegrams from –

Mae (*at same time*)   What is it, Brick?

Gooper   I bet 500 to 50 that Brick don't *know* what it is.

Big Mama   The fun of presents is not knowing what they are till you open the package. Open your present, Big Daddy.

Big Daddy   Open it you'self. I want to ask Brick somethin! Come here, Brick.

Margaret   Big Daddy's callin' you, Brick.

She is opening the package.

Brick   Tell Big Daddy I'm crippled.

Big Daddy   I see you're crippled. I want to know how you got crippled.

Margaret (*making diversionary tactics*)   *Oh, look, oh, look, why, it's a cashmere robe!*

She holds the robe up for all to see.

Mae   You sound surprised, Maggie.

Margaret   I never saw one before.

Mae   That's funny. – *Hah!*

Margaret (*turning on her fiercely, with a brilliant smile*)   Why is it funny? All my family ever had was family – and luxuries such as cashmere robes still surprise me!

Big Daddy (*ominously*)   Quiet!

Mae (*heedless in her fury*)   I don't see how you could be so surprised when you bought it yourself at Loewenstein's in Memphis last Saturday. You know how I know?

Big Daddy   I said, Quiet!

Mae   – I know because the salesgirl that sold it to you waited on me and said, Oh, Mrs Pollitt, your sister-in-law just bought a cashmere robe for your husband's father!

Margaret   Sister Woman! Your talents are wasted as a housewife and mother, you really ought to be with the FBI or –

Big Daddy   QUIET!

Reverend Tooker's *reflexes are slower than the others'. He finishes a sentence after the bellow.*

Reverend Tooker (*to* **Doc Baugh**)   – the Stork and the Reaper are running neck and neck!

He starts to laugh gaily when he notices the silence and **Big Daddy**'s *glare. His laugh dies falsely.*

Big Daddy   Preacher, I hope I'm not butting in on more talk about memorial stained-glass windows, am I, Preacher?

Reverend Tooker *laughs feebly, then coughs dryly in the embarrassed silence.*

Big Daddy   Preacher?

Big Mama   Now, Big Daddy, don't you pick on Preacher!

Big Daddy (*raising his voice*)   You ever hear that expression all hawk and no spit? You bring that expression to mind with that little dry cough of yours, all hawk an' no spit . . .

The pause is broken only by a short startled laugh from **Margaret***, the only one there who is conscious of and amused by the grotesque.*

Mae (*raising her arms and jangling her bracelets*)   I wonder if the mosquitoes are active tonight?

Big Daddy   What's that, Little Mama? Did you make some remark?

Mae   Yes, I said I wondered if the mosquitoes would eat us alive if we went out on the gallery for a while.

Big Daddy   Well, if they do, I'll have your bones pulverized for fertilizer!

Big Mama (*quickly*)   Last week we had an airplane spraying the place and I think it done some good, at least I haven't had a –

Big Daddy (*cutting her speech*)   Brick, they tell me, if what they tell me is true, that you done some jumping last night on the high school athletic field?

Big Mama   Brick, Big Daddy is talking to you, son.

Brick (*smiling vaguely over his drink*)   What was that, Big Daddy?

Big Daddy   They said you done some jumping on the high school track field last night.

Brick   That's what they told me, too.

Big Daddy   Was it jumping or humping that you were doing out there? What were doing out there at three a.m., layin' a woman on that cinder track?

Big Mama   Big Daddy, you are off the sick-list, now, and I'm not going to excuse you for talkin' so –

Big Daddy   Quiet!

Big Mama   – *nasty* in front of Preacher and –

Big Daddy   *QUIET!* – I ast you, Brick, if you was cuttin' you'self a piece o' poon-tang last night on that cinder track? I thought maybe you were chasin' poon-tang on that track an' tripped over something in the heat of the chase – 's that it?

Gooper *laughs, loud and false, others nervously following suit.* **Big Mama** *stamps her foot, and purses her lips, crossing to* **Mae** *and whispering something to her as* **Brick** *meets his father's hard, intent, grinning stare with a slow, vague smile that he offers all situations from behind the screen of his liquor.*

Brick   No, sir, I don't think so . . .

Mae (*at the same time, sweetly*)   Reverend Tooker, let's you and I take a stroll on the widow's walk.

She and the preacher go out on the gallery as **Big Daddy** *says:*

Big Daddy   Then what the hell were you doing out there at three o'clock in the morning?

Brick   Jumping the hurdles, Big Daddy, runnin' and jumpin' the hurdles, but those high hurdles have gotten too high for me, now.

Big Daddy   'Cause you was drunk?

Brick (*his vague smile fading a little*)   Sober I wouldn't have tried to jump the *low* ones . . .

Big Mama (*quickly*)   Big Daddy, blow out the candles on your birthday cake!

Margaret (*at the same time*)   I want to propose a toast to Big Daddy Pollitt on his sixty-fifth birthday, the biggest cotton planter in –

Big Daddy (*bellowing with fury and disgust*)   *I told you to stop it, now stop it, quit this– !*

Big Mama (*coming in front of* **Big Daddy** *with the cake*)   Big Daddy, I will not allow you to talk that way, not even on your birthday, I –

Big Daddy   I'll talk like I want to on my birthday, Ida, or any other goddam day of the year and anybody here that don't like it knows what they can do!

Big Mama   You don't mean that!

Big Daddy   What makes you think I don't mean it?

Meanwhile various discreet signals have been exchanged and **Gooper** *has also gone out on the gallery.*

Big Mama   I just know you don't mean it.

Big Daddy   You don't know a goddam thing and you never did!

Big Mama   Big Daddy, you don't mean that.

Big Daddy   Oh, yes, I do, oh, yes, I do, I mean it! I put up with a whole lot of crap around here because I thought I was dying. And you thought I was dying and you started taking over, well, you can stop taking over now, Ida, because I'm not gonna die, you can just stop now this business of taking over because you're not taking over because I'm not dying, I went through the laboratory and the goddam exploratory operation and there's nothing wrong with me but a spastic colon. And I'm not dying of cancer which you thought I was dying of. Ain't that so? Didn't you think that I was dying of cancer, Ida?

Almost everybody is out on the gallery but the two old people glaring at each other across the blazing cake.

Big Mama*'s chest heaves and she presses a fat fist to her mouth.*

Big Daddy *continues, hoarsely:*

Big Daddy   Ain't that so, Ida? Didn't you have an idea I was dying of cancer and now you could take control of this place and everything on it? I got that impression, I seemed to get that impression. Your loud voice everywhere, your fat old body butting in here and there!

Big Mama   Hush! The Preacher!

Big Daddy   Fuck the goddam preacher!

Big Mama *gasps loudly and sits down on the sofa which is almost too small for her.*

Big Daddy   Did you hear what I said? I said fuck the goddam preacher!

Somebody closes the gallery doors from outside just as there is a burst of fireworks and excited cries from the children.

Big Mama   I never seen you act like this before and I can't think what's got in you!

Big Daddy   I went through all that laboratory and operation and all just so I would know if you or me was boss here! Well, now it turns out that I am and you ain't – and that's my birthday present – and my cake and champagne! – because for three years now you been gradually taking over. Bossing. Talking. Sashaying your fat old body around the place I made! I made this place! I was overseer on it! I was the overseer on the old Straw and Ochello plantation. I quit school at ten! I quit school at ten years old and went to work like a nigger in the fields. And I rose to be overseer of the Straw and Ochello plantation. And old Straw died and I was Ochello's partner and the place got bigger and bigger and bigger and bigger and bigger! I did all that myself with no goddam help from you, and now you think you're just about to take over. Well, I am just about to tell you that you are not just about to take over, you are not just about to take over a God damn thing. Is that clear to you, Ida? Is that very plain to you, now? Is that understood completely? I been through the laboratory from A to Z. I've had the goddam exploratory operation, and nothing is wrong with me but a spastic colon – made spastic, I guess, by *disgust*! By all the goddam lies and liars that I have had to put up with, and all the goddam hypocrisy that I lived with all these forty years that we been livin' together!

Hey! Ida!! Blow out the candles on the birthday cake! Purse up your lips and draw a deep breath and blow out the goddam candles on the cake!

Big Mama   Oh, Big Daddy, oh, oh, oh, Big Daddy!

Big Daddy   What's the matter with you?

Big Mama   *In all these years you never believed that I loved you??*

Big Daddy   Huh?

Big Mama   *And I did, I did so much, I did love you!* – I even loved your hate and your hardness, Big Daddy!

She sobs and rushes awkwardly out onto the gallery.

Big Daddy (*to himself*)   *Wouldn't it be funny if that was true . . .*

A pause is followed by a burst of light in the sky from the fireworks.

Big Daddy   *BRICK! HEY, BRICK!*

He stands over his blazing birthday cake.

After some moments, **Brick** *hobbles in on his crutch, holding his glass.*

Margaret *follows him with a bright, anxious smile.*

Big Daddy   I didn't call you, Maggie. I called Brick.

Margaret   I'm just delivering him to you.

She kisses **Brick** *on the mouth which he immediately wipes with the back of his hand. She flies girlishly back out.* **Brick** *and his father are alone.*

Big Daddy   Why did you do that?

Brick   Do what, Big Daddy?

Big Daddy   Wipe her kiss off your mouth like she'd spit on you.

Brick   I don't know. I wasn't conscious of it.

Big Daddy   That woman of yours has a better shape on her than Gooper's but somehow or other they got the same look about them.

Brick   What sort of look is that, Big Daddy?

Big Daddy   I don't know how to describe it but it's the same look.

Brick   They don't look peaceful, do they?

Big Daddy   No, they sure in hell don't.

Brick   They look nervous as cats?

Big Daddy   That's right, they look nervous as cats.

Brick   Nervous as a couple of cats on a hot tin roof?

Big Daddy   That's right, boy, they look like a couple of cats on a hot tin roof. It's funny that you and Gooper being so different would pick out the same type of woman.

Brick   Both of us married into society, Big Daddy.

Big Daddy   Crap . . . I wonder what gives them both that look?

Brick   Well. They're sittin' in the middle of a big piece of land, Big Daddy, twenty-eight thousand acres is a pretty big piece of land and so they're squaring off on it, each determined to knock off a bigger piece of it than the other whenever you let it go.

Big Daddy   I got a surprise for those women. I'm not gonna let it go for a long time yet if that's what they're waiting for.

Brick   That's right, Big Daddy. You just sit tight and let them scratch each other's eyes out . . .

Big Daddy   You bet your life I'm going to sit tight on it and let those sons of bitches scratch their eyes out, ha ha ha . . .

But Gooper's wife's a good breeder, you got to admit she's fertile. Hell, at supper tonight she had them all at the table and they had to put a couple of extra leafs in the table to make room for them, she's got five head of them, now, and another one's comin'.

Brick Yep, number six is comin' . . .

Big Daddy Six hell, she'll probably drop a litter next time. Brick, you know, I swear to God, I don't know the way it happens?

Brick The way what happens, Big Daddy?

Big Daddy You git you a piece of land, by hook or crook, an' things start growin' on it, things accumulate on it, and the first thing you know it's completely out of hand, completely out of hand!

Brick Well, they say nature hates a vacuum, Big Daddy.

Big Daddy That's what they say, but sometimes I think that a vacuum is a hell of a lot better than some of the stuff that nature replaces it with.

Is someone out there by that door?

Gooper Hey Mae.

Brick Yep.

Big Daddy Who?

He has lowered his voice.

Brick Someone int'rested in what we say to each other.

Big Daddy Gooper? – *GOOPER!*

After a discreet pause, **Mae** *appears in the gallery door.*

Mae Did you call Gooper, Big Daddy?

Big Daddy Aw, it was you.

Mae Do you want Gooper, Big Daddy?

Big Daddy   No, and I don't want you. I want some privacy here, while I'm having a confidential talk with my son Brick. Now it's too hot in here to close them doors, but if I have to close those fuckin' doors in order to have a private talk with my son Brick, just let me know and I'll close 'em. Because I hate eavesdroppers, I don't like any kind of sneakin' an' spyin'.

Mae   Why, Big Daddy –

Big Daddy   You stood on the wrong side of the moon, it threw your shadow!

Mae   I was just –

Big Daddy   You was just nothing but *spyin'* an' you *know* it!

Mae (*begins to sniff and sob*)   Oh, Big Daddy, you're so unkind for some reason to those that really love you!

Big Daddy   Shut up, shut up, shut up! I'm going to move you and Gooper out of that room next to this! It's none of your goddam business what goes on in here at night between Brick an' Maggie. You listen at night like a couple of rutten peekhole spies and go and give a report on what you hear to Big Mama an' she comes to me and says they say such and such and so and so about what they heard goin' on between Brick an' Maggie, and Jesus, it makes me sick. I'm goin' to move you an' Gooper out of that room, I can't stand sneakin' an' spyin', it makes me puke . . .

Mae *throws back her head and rolls her eyes heavenward and extends her arms as if invoking God's pity for this unjust martyrdom; then she presses a handkerchief to her nose and flies from the room with a loud swish of skirts.*

Brick (*now at the liquor cabinet*)   They listen, do they?

Big Daddy   Yeah. They listen and give reports to Big Mama on what goes on in here between you and Maggie. They say that –

He stops as if embarrassed.

– You won't sleep with her, that you sleep on the sofa. Is that true or not true? If you don't like Maggie, get rid of Maggie! – What are you doin' there now?

Brick   Fresh'nin' up my drink.

Big Daddy   Son, you know you got a real liquor problem?

Brick   Yes, sir, yes, I know.

Big Daddy   Is that why you quit sports-announcing, because of this liquor problem?

Brick   Yes, sir, yes, sir, I guess so.

He smiles vaguely and amiably at his father across his replenished drink.

Big Daddy   Son, don't guess about it, it's too important.

Brick (*vaguely*)   Yes, sir.

Big Daddy   And listen to me, don't look at the damn chandelier . . .

Pause. **Big Daddy**'s *voice is husky.*

– Somethin' else we picked up at th' big fire sale in Europe.

Another pause.

Life is important. There's nothing else to hold onto. A man that drinks is throwing his life away. Don't do it, hold onto your life. There's nothing else to hold onto . . .

Sit down over here so we don't have to raise our voices, the walls have ears in this place.

Brick (*hobbling over to sit on the sofa beside him*)   All right, Big Daddy.

Big Daddy   Quit! – how'd that come about? Some disappointment?

Brick   I don't know. Do you?

Big Daddy   I'm askin' you, God damn it! How in hell would I know if you don't?

Brick I just got out there and found that I had a mouth full of cotton. I was always two or three beats behind what was goin' on on the field and so I –

Big Daddy Quit!

Brick (*amiably*) Yes, quit.

Big Daddy Son?

Brick Huh?

Big Daddy (*inhales loudly and deeply from his cigar; then bends suddenly a little forward, exhaling loudly and raising a hand to his forehead*) – Whew! – ha ha! – I took in too much smoke, it made me a little lightheaded . . .

The mantel clock chimes.

Why is it so damn hard for people to talk?

Brick Yeah . . .

The clock goes on sweetly chiming till it has completed the stroke of ten.

– Nice peaceful-soundin' clock, I like to hear it all night . . .

He slides low and comfortable on the sofa; **Big Daddy** *sits up straight and rigid with some unspoken anxiety. All his gestures are tense and jerky as he talks. He wheezes and pants and sniffs through his nervous speech, glancing quickly, shyly, from time to time, at his son.*

Big Daddy We got that clock the summer we wint to Europe, me an' Big Mama on that damn Cook's Tour, never had such an awful time in my life, I'm tellin' you, son, those gooks over there, they gouge your eyeballs out in their grand hotels. And Big Mama bought more stuff than you could haul in a couple of boxcars, that's no crap. Everywhere she wint on this whirlwind tour, she bought, bought, bought. Why, half that stuff she bought is still crated up in the cellar, under water last spring!

He laughs.

That Europe is nothin' on earth but a great big auction, that's all it is, that bunch of old worn-out places, it's just a big fire sale, the whole fuckin' thing, an' Big Mama wint wild in it, why, you couldn't hold that woman with a mule's harness! Bought, bought, bought! – lucky I'm a rich man, yes siree, Bob, an' half that stuff is mildewin' in th' basement. It's lucky I'm a rich man, it sure is lucky, well, I'm a rich man, Brick, yep, I'm a mighty rich man.

His eyes light up for a moment.

Y'know how much I'm worth? Guess, Brick! Guess how much I'm worth!

Brick *smiles vaguely over his drink.*

Big Daddy   Close on ten million in cash an' blue-chip stocks, outside, mind you, of twenty-eight thousand acres of the richest land this side of the valley Nile!

But a man can't buy his life with it, he can't buy back his life with it when his life has been spent, that's one thing not offered in the Europe fire-sale or in the American markets or any markets on earth, a man can't buy his life with it, he can't buy back his life when his life is finished . . .

That's a sobering thought, a very sobering thought, and that's a thought that I was turning over in my head, over and over and over – until today . . .

I'm wiser and sadder, Brick, for this experience which I just gone through. They's one thing else that I remember in Europe.

Brick   What is that, Big Daddy?

Big Daddy   The hills around Barcelona in the country of Spain and the children running over those bare hills in their bare skins beggin' like starvin' dogs with howls and screeches, and how fat the priests are on the streets of Barcelona, so many of them and so fat and so pleasant, ha ha! – Y'know I could feed that country? I got money enough to feed that goddam country, but the human animal is a selfish beast and I don't reckon the money I passed out there to those howling children in the hills around Barcelona would more than upholster the chairs in this room, I mean pay to put a new cover on this chair!

Hell, I threw them money like you'd scatter feed corn for chickens, I threw money at them just to get rid of them long enough to climb back into th' car and – drive away . . .

And then in Morocco, them Arabs, why, I remember one day in Marrakech, that old walled Arab city, I set on a broken-down wall to have a cigar, it was fearful hot there and this Arab woman stood in the road and looked at me till I was embarrassed, she stood stock still in the dusty hot road and looked at me till I was embarrassed. But listen to this. She had a naked child with her, a little naked girl with her, barely able to toddle, and after a while she set this child on the ground and give her a push and whispered something to her.

This child come toward me, barely able t' walk, come toddling up to me and –

Jesus, it makes you sick t' remember a thing like this! It stuck out its hand and tried to unbutton my trousers!

That child was not yet five! Can you believe me? Or do you think that I am making this up? I wint back to the hotel and said to Big Mama, Git packed! We're clearing out of this country . . .

Brick   Big Daddy, you're on a talkin' jag tonight.

Big Daddy (*ignoring this remark*)   Yes, sir, that's how it is, the human animal is a beast that dies but the fact that he's dying don't give him pity for others, no, sir, it –

– Did you say something?

Brick   Yes.

Big Daddy   What?

Brick   Hand me over that crutch so I can get up.

Big Daddy   Where you goin'?

Brick   I'm takin' a little short trip to Echo Spring.

Big Daddy   To where?

Brick   Liquor cabinet . . .

Big Daddy   Yes, sir, boy –

*He hands **Brick** the crutch.*

– the human animal is a beast that dies and if he's got money he buys and buys and buys and I think the reason he buys everything he can buy is that in the back of his mind he has the crazy hope that one of his purchases will be life everlasting! – Which it never can be . . . The human animal is a beast that –

Brick (*at the liquor cabinet*)   Big Daddy, you sure are shootin' th' breeze here tonight.

There is a pause and voices are heard outside.

Big Daddy   I been quiet here lately, spoke not a word, just sat and stared into space. I had something heavy weighing on my mind but tonight that load was took off me. That's why I'm talking. The sky looks diff'rent to me . . .

Brick   You know what I like to hear most?

Big Daddy   What?

Brick   Solid quiet. Perfect unbroken quiet.

Big Daddy   Why?

Brick   Because it's more peaceful.

Big Daddy   Man, you'll hear a lot of that in the grave.

He chuckles agreeably.

Brick   Are you through talkin' to me?

Big Daddy   Why are you so anxious to shut me up?

Brick   Well, sir, ever so often you say to me, Brick, I want to have a talk with you, but when we talk, it never materializes. Nothing is said. You sit in a chair and gas about this and that and I look like I listen. I try to look like I listen, but I don't listen, not much. Communication is – awful hard between people an' – somehow between you and me, it just don't – happen.

Big Daddy   Have you ever been scared? I mean have you ever felt downright terror of something?

He gets up.

Just one moment.

He looks off as if he were going to tell an important secret.

Brick?

Brick   What?

Big Daddy   Son, I thought I had it!

Brick   Had what? Had what, Big Daddy?

Big Daddy   Cancer!

Brick   Oh . . .

Big Daddy   I thought the old man made out of bones had laid his cold and heavy hand on my shoulder!

Brick   Well, Big Daddy, you kept a tight mouth about it.

Big Daddy   A pig squeals. A man keeps a tight mouth about it, in spite of a man not having a pig's advantage.

Brick   What advantage is that?

Big Daddy   Ignorance – of mortality – is a comfort. A man don't have that comfort, he's the only living thing that conceives of death, that knows what it is. The others go without knowing which is the way that anything living should go, go without knowing, without any knowledge of it, and yet a pig squeals, but a man sometimes, he can keep a tight mouth about it. Sometimes he –

There is a deep, smoldering ferocity in the old man.

– can keep a tight mouth about it. I wonder if –

Brick   What, Big Daddy?

Big Daddy   A whiskey highball would injure this spastic condition?

Brick   No, sir, it might do it good.

Big Daddy (*grins suddenly, wolfishly*) *Jesus, I can't tell you! The sky is open! Christ, it's open again! It's open, boy, it's open!*

Brick *looks down at his drink.*

Brick   You feel better, Big Daddy?

Big Daddy   Better? Hell! I can breathe! – All of my life I been like a doubled-up fist . . .

He pours a drink.

– Poundin', smashin', drivin'! – now I'm going to loosen these doubled-up hands and touch things *easy* with them . . .

He spreads his hands as if caressing the air.

You know what I'm contemplating?

Brick (*vaguely*)   No, sir. What are you contemplating?

Big Daddy   Ha ha! – *Pleasure!* – pleasure with *women*!

Brick's *smile fades a little but lingers.*

Big Daddy   – Yes, boy. I'll tell you something that you might not guess. I still have desire for women and this is my sixty-fifth birthday.

Brick   I think that's mighty remarkable, Big Daddy.

Big Daddy   Remarkable?

Brick   *Admirable*, Big Daddy.

Big Daddy   You're damn right it is, remarkable and admirable both. I realize now that I never had me enough. I let many chances slip by because of scruples about it, scruples, convention – crap . . . All that stuff is bull, bull, bull! – It took the shadow of death to make me see it. Now that shadow's lifted, I'm going to cut loose and have, what is it they call it, have me a – ball!

Brick   A ball, huh?

Big Daddy   That's right, a ball, a ball! Hell! – I slept with Big Mama till, let's see, five years ago, till I was sixty and she was fifty-eight, and never even liked her, never did!

The phone has been ringing down the hall. **Big Mama** *enters, exclaiming:*

Big Mama   Don't you men hear that phone ring? I heard it way out on the gall'ry.

Big Daddy   There's five rooms off this front gall'ry that you could go through. Why do you go through this one?

Big Mama *makes a playful face as she bustles out the hall door.*

Big Daddy   Hunh! – Why, when Big Mama goes out of a room, I can't remember what that woman looks like –

Big Mama   Hello.

Big Daddy   – But when Big Mama comes back into the room, boy, then I see what she looks like, and I wish I didn't!

Bends over laughing at this joke till it hurts his guts and he straightens with a grimace. The laugh subsides to a chuckle as he puts the liquor glass a little distrustfully down on the table.

Big Mama   Hello, Miss Sally.

Brick *has risen and hobbled to the gallery doors.*

Big Daddy   Hey! Where you goin'?

Brick   Out for a breather.

Big Daddy   Not yet you ain't. Stay here till this talk is finished, young fellow.

Brick   I thought it was finished, Big Daddy.

Big Daddy   It ain't even begun.

Brick   My mistake. Excuse me. I just wanted to feel that river breeze.

Big Daddy   Set back down in that chair.

Big Mama's *voice rises, carrying down the hall.*

Big Mama   Miss Sally, you're a case! You're a caution, Miss Sally.

Big Daddy   Jesus, she's talking to my old maid sister again.

Big Mama   Why didn't you give me a chance to explain it to you?

Big Daddy   Brick, this stuff burns me.

Big Mama   Well, goodbye, now, Miss Sally. You come down real soon. Big Daddy's dying to see you.

Big Daddy   Crap!

Big Mama   Yaiss, goodbye, Miss Sally . . .

She hangs up and bellows with mirth. **Big Daddy** *groans and covers his ears as she approaches.*

Bursting in:

Big Mama   Big Daddy, that was Miss Sally callin' from Memphis again! You know what she done, Big Daddy? She called her doctor in Memphis to git him to tell her what that spastic thing is! Ha-*HAAAA!* – And called back to tell me how relieved she was that – Hey! Let me in!

Big Daddy *has been holding the door half closed against her.*

Big Daddy   Naw I ain't. I told you not to come and go through this room. You just back out and go through those five other rooms.

Big Mama   Big Daddy? Big Daddy? Oh, Big Daddy! – You didn't mean those things you said to me, did you?

He shuts door firmly against her but she still calls.

Sweetheart? Sweetheart? Big Daddy? You didn't mean those awful things you said to me? – I know you didn't. I know you didn't mean those things in your heart . . .

The childlike voice fades with a sob and her heavy footsteps retreat down the hall. **Brick** *has risen once more on his crutches and starts for the gallery again.*

Big Daddy   All I ask of that woman is that she leave me alone. But she can't admit to herself that she makes me sick. That comes of having slept with her too many years. Should of quit much sooner but that old woman she never got enough of it – and I was good in bed . . . I never should of wasted so much of it on her . . . They say you got just so many and each one is numbered. Well, I got a few left in me, a few, and I'm going to pick me a good one to spend 'em on! I'm going to pick me a choice one, I don't care how much she costs, I'll smother her in – minks! Ha ha! I'll strip her naked and smother her in minks and choke her with diamonds! Ha ha! I'll strip her naked and choke her with diamonds and smother her with minks and hump her from hell to breakfast. *Ha aha ha ha ha!*

Mae (*gaily at door*)   Who's that laughin' in there?

Gooper   Is Big Daddy laughin' in there?

Big Daddy   Crap! – them two – *drips* . . .

He goes over and touches **Brick**'*s shoulder.*

Big Daddy   Yes, son. Brick, boy. – I'm – *happy!* I'm happy, son, I'm happy!

He chokes a little and bites his under lip, pressing his head quickly, shyly against his son's head and then, coughing with embarrassment, goes uncertainly back to the table where he set down the glass. He drinks and makes a grimace as it burns his guts. **Brick** *sighs and rises with effort.*

Big Daddy   What makes you so restless? Have you got ants in your britches?

Brick   Yes, sir . . .

Big Daddy   Why?

Brick   – Something – hasn't – happened . . .

Big Daddy   Yeah? What is that!

Brick (*sadly*)   – the click . . .

Big Daddy   Did you say click?

Brick   Yes, click.

Big Daddy   What click?

Brick   A click that I get in my head that makes me peaceful.

Big Daddy   I sure in hell don't know what you're talking about, but it disturbs me.

Brick   It's just a mechanical thing.

Big Daddy   What is a mechanical thing?

Brick   This click that I get in my head that makes me peaceful. I got to drink till I get it. It's just a mechanical thing, something like a – like a – like a –

Big Daddy   Like a –

Brick   Switch clicking off in my head, turning the hot light off and the cool night on and –

He looks up, smiling sadly.

– all of a sudden there's – peace!

Big Daddy (*whistles long and soft with astonishment; he goes back to* **Brick** *and clasps his son's two shoulders*)   Jesus! I didn't know it had gotten that bad with you. Why, boy, you're – *alcoholic*!

Brick   That's the truth, Big Daddy. I'm alcoholic.

Big Daddy   This shows how I – let things go!

Brick   I have to hear that little click in my head that makes me peaceful. Usually I hear it sooner than this, sometimes as early as – noon, but –

– Today it's – dilatory . . .

– I just haven't got the right level of alcohol in my bloodstream yet!

This last statement is made with energy as he freshens his drink.

Big Daddy   Uh-huh. Expecting death made me blind.
I didn't have no idea that a son of mine was turning into a
drunkard under my nose.

Brick (*gently*)   Well, now you do, Big Daddy, the news has
penetrated.

Big Daddy   UH-huh, yes, now I do, the news has –
penetrated . . .

Brick   And so if you'll excuse me –

Big Daddy   No, I won't excuse you.

Brick   – I'd better sit by myself till I hear that click in my
head, it's just a mechanical thing but it don't happen except
when I'm alone or talking to no one . . .

Big Daddy   You got a long, long time to sit still, boy, and
talk to no one, but now you're talkin' to me. At least I'm
talking to you. And you set there and listen until I tell you the
conversation is over!

Brick   But this talk is like all the others we've ever had
together in our lives! It's nowhere, nowhere! – it's – it's *painful*,
Big Daddy . . .

Big Daddy   All right, then let it be painful, but don't you
move from that chair! – I'm going to remove that crutch . . .

He seizes the crutch and tosses it across room.

Brick   I can hop on one foot, and if I fall, I can crawl!

Big Daddy   If you ain't careful you're gonna crawl off this
plantation and then, by Jesus, you'll have to hustle your drinks
along Skid Row!

Brick   That'll come, Big Daddy.

Big Daddy   Naw, it won't. You're my son and I'm going to
straighten you out; now that *I'm* straightened out, I'm going to
straighten out you!

Brick   Yeah?

Big Daddy   Today the report come in from Ochsner Clinic. Y'know what they told me?

His face glows with triumph.

The only thing that they could detect with all the instruments of science in that great hospital is a little spastic condition of the colon! And nerves torn to pieces by all that worry about it.

A little girl bursts into room with a sparkler clutched in each fist, hops and shrieks like a monkey gone mad and rushes back out again as **Big Daddy** *strikes at her.*

Silence. The two men stare at each other. A woman laughs gaily outside.

I want you to know I breathed a sigh of relief almost as powerful as the Vicksburg tornado!

There is laughter outside, running footsteps, the soft, plushy sound and light of exploding rockets.

Brick *stares at him soberly for a long moment; then makes a sort of startled sound in his nostrils and springs up on one foot and hops across the room to grab his crutch, swinging on the furniture for support. He gets the crutch and flees as if in horror for the gallery. His father seizes him by the sleeve of his white silk pajamas.*

Big Daddy   Stay here, you son of a bitch! – till I say go!

Brick   I can't.

Big Daddy   You sure in hell will, God damn it.

Brick   No, I can't. We talk, you talk, in – circles! We get nowhere, nowhere! It's always the same, you say you want to talk to me and don't have a fuckin' thing to say to me!

Big Daddy   Nothin' to say when I'm tellin' you I'm going to live when I thought I was dying?!

Brick   Oh – *that!* – Is that what you have to say to me?

Big Daddy   Why, you son of a bitch! Ain't that, ain't that – *important?!*

Brick   Well, you said that, that's said, and now I –

Big Daddy   Now you set back down.

Brick   You're all balled up, you –

Big Daddy   I ain't balled up!

Brick   You are, you're all balled up!

Big Daddy   Don't tell me what I am, you drunken whelp! I'm going to tear this coat sleeve off if you don't set down!

Brick   Big Daddy –

Big Daddy   Do what I tell you! I'm the boss here, now! I want you to know I'm back in the driver's seat now!

Big Mama *rushes in, clutching her great heaving bosom.*

Big Mama   Big Daddy!

Big Daddy   What in hell do you want in here, Big Mama?

Big Mama   Oh, Big Daddy! Why are you shouting like that? I just cain't *stainnnnnnnd – it* . . .

Big Daddy (*raising the back of his hand above his head*)   *GIT!* – outa here.

She rushes back out, sobbing.

Brick (*softly, sadly*)   *Christ* . . .

Big Daddy (*fiercely*)   Yeah! Christ! – is right . . .

Brick *breaks loose and hobbles toward the gallery.*

Big Daddy *jerks his crutch from under* **Brick** *so he steps with the injured ankle. He utters a hissing cry of anguish, clutches a chair and pulls it over on top of him on the floor.*

Big Daddy   Son of a – tub of – hog fat . . .

Brick   Big Daddy! Give me my crutch.

Big Daddy *throws the crutch out of reach.*

Brick   Give me that crutch, Big Daddy.

Big Daddy   Why do you drink?

Brick   Don't know, give me my crutch!

Big Daddy   You better think why you drink or give up drinking!

Brick   Will you please give me my crutch so I can get up off this floor?

Big Daddy   First you answer my question. Why do you drink? Why are you throwing your life away, boy, like somethin' disgusting you picked up on the street?

Brick (*getting onto his knees*)   Big Daddy, I'm in pain, I stepped on that foot.

Big Daddy   Good! I'm glad you're not too numb with the liquor in you to feel some pain!

Brick   You – spilled my – drink . . .

Big Daddy   I'll make a bargain with you. You tell me why you drink and I'll hand you one. I'll pour you the liquor myself and hand it to you.

Brick   Why do I drink?

Big Daddy   Yeah! Why?

Brick   Give me a drink and I'll tell you.

Big Daddy   Tell me first!

Brick   I'll tell you in one word.

Big Daddy   What word?

Brick   DISGUST!

The clock chimes softly, sweetly. **Big Daddy** *gives it a short, outraged glance.*

Brick   Now how about that drink?

Big Daddy   What are you disgusted with? You got to tell me that, first. Otherwise being disgusted don't make no sense!

Brick   Give me my crutch.

Big Daddy   You heard me, you got to tell me what I asked you first.

Brick   I told you, I said to kill my disgust!

Big Daddy   DISGUST WITH WHAT!

Brick   You strike a hard bargain.

Big Daddy   What are you disgusted with? – an' I'll pass you the liquor.

Brick   I can hop on one foot, and if I fall, I can crawl.

Big Daddy   You want liquor that bad?

Brick (*dragging himself up, clinging to bedstead*)   Yeah, I want it that bad.

Big Daddy   If I give you a drink, will you tell me what it is you're disgusted with, Brick?

Brick   Yes, sir, I will try to.

The old man pours him a drink and solemnly passes it to him.

There is silence as **Brick** *drinks.*

Have you ever heard the word 'mendacity'?

Big Daddy   Sure. Mendacity is one of them five dollar words that cheap politicians throw back and forth at each other.

Brick   You know what it means?

Big Daddy   Don't it mean lying and liars?

Brick   Yes, sir, lying and liars.

Big Daddy   Has someone been lying to you?

Children (*chanting in chorus offstage*)
   We want Big Dad-dee!
   We want Big Dad-dee!

Gooper *appears in the gallery door.*

Gooper   Big Daddy, the kiddies are shouting for you out there.

Big Daddy (*fiercely*)   Keep out, Gooper!

Gooper   'Scuse *me*!

Big Daddy *slams the doors after* **Gooper**.

Big Daddy   Who's been lying to you, has Margaret been lying to you, has your wife been lying to you about something, Brick?

Brick   Not her. That wouldn't matter.

Big Daddy   Then who's been lying to you, and what about?

Brick   No one single person and no one lie . . .

Big Daddy   Then what, what then, for Christ's sake?

Brick   – The whole, the whole – thing . . .

Big Daddy   Why are you rubbing your head? You got a headache?

Brick   No, I'm tryin' to –

Big Daddy   – Concentrate, but you can't because your brain's all soaked with liquor, is that the trouble? Wet brain!

He snatches the glass from **Brick***'s hand.*

Big Daddy   What do you know about this mendacity thing? Hell! I could write a book on it! Don't you know that? I could write a book on it and still not cover the subject? Well, I could, I could write a goddam book on it and still not cover the subject anywhere near enough!! – Think of all the lies I got to put up with! – Pretenses! Ain't that mendacity? Having to pretend stuff you don't think or feel or have any idea of? Having for instance to act like I care for Big Mama! – I haven't been able to stand the sight, sound, or smell of that woman for forty years now! – even when I *laid* her! – regular as a piston . . .

Pretend to love that son of a bitch of a Gooper and his wife
Mae and those five same screechers out there like parrots in a
jungle? Jesus! Can't stand to look at 'em!

Church! – it bores the bejesus out of me but I go! – I go an' sit
there and listen to the fool preacher!

Clubs! – Elks! Masons! Rotary! – *crap!*

*A spasm of pain makes him clutch his belly. He sinks into a chair and
his voice is softer and hoarser.*

You I *do* like for some reason, did always have some kind of real
feeling for – affection – respect – yes, always . . .

You and being a success as a planter is all I ever had any
devotion to in my whole life! – and that's the truth . . .

I don't know why, but it is!

I've lived with mendacity! – Why can't *you* live with it? Hell,
you *got* to live with it, there's nothing *else* to *live* with except
mendacity, is there?

Brick   Yes, sir. Yes, sir there is something else that you can
live with!

Big Daddy   What?

Brick (*lifting his glass*)   This! – Liquor . . .

Big Daddy   That's not living, that's dodging away from life.

Brick   I want to dodge away from it.

Big Daddy   Then why don't you kill yourself, man?

Brick   I like to drink . . .

Big Daddy   Oh, God, I can't talk to you . . .

Brick   I'm sorry, Big Daddy.

Big Daddy   Not as sorry as I am. I'll tell you something.
A little while back when I thought my number was up –

This speech should have torrential pace and fury.

– before I found out it was just this – spastic – colon. I thought about you. Should I or should I not, if the jig was up, give you this place when I go – since I hate Gooper an' Mae an' know that they hate me, and since all five same monkeys are little Maes an' Goopers. – And I thought, No! – Then I thought, Yes! – I couldn't make up my mind. I hate Gooper and his five same monkeys and that bitch Mae! Why should I turn over twenty-eight thousand acres of the richest land this side of the valley Nile to not my kind? – But why in hell, on the other hand, Brick – should I subsidize a goddam fool on the bottle? – liked or not liked, well, maybe even – *loved*! – Why should I do that? – Subsidize worthless behavior? Rot? Corruption?

Brick (*smiling*)   I understand.

Big Daddy   Well, if you do, you're smarter than I am, God damn it, because I don't understand. And this I will tell you frankly. I didn't make up my mind at all on that question and still to this day I ain't made out no will! – Well, now I don't *have* to. The pressure is gone. I can just wait and see if you pull yourself together or if you don't.

Brick   That's right, Big Daddy.

Big Daddy   You sound like you thought I was kidding.

Brick (*rising*)   No, sir, I know you're not kidding.

Big Daddy   But you don't care – ?

Brick (*hobbling toward the gallery door*)   No, sir, I don't care . . .

He stands in the gallery doorway as the night sky turns pink and green and gold with successive flashes of light.

Big Daddy   *WAIT!* – Brick . . .

His voice drops. Suddenly there is something shy, almost tender, in his restraining gesture.

Don't let's – leave it like this, like them other talks we've had, we've always – talked around things, we've – just talked around things for some fuckin' reason, I don't know what, it's always like something was left not spoken, something avoided because neither of us was honest enough with the − other . . .

Brick   I never lied to you, Big Daddy.

Big Daddy   Did I ever to *you*?

Brick   No, sir . . .

Big Daddy   Then there is at least two people that never lied to each other.

Brick   But we've never *talked* to each other.

Big Daddy   We can *now.*

Brick   Big Daddy, there don't seem to be anything much to say.

Big Daddy   You say that you drink to kill your disgust with lying.

Brick   You said to give you a reason.

Big Daddy   Is liquor the only thing that'll kill this disgust?

Brick   Now. Yes.

Big Daddy   But not once, huh?

Brick   Not when I was still young an' believing. A drinking man's someone who wants to forget he isn't still young an' believing.

Big Daddy   Believing what?

Brick   Believing . . .

Big Daddy   Believing *what*?

Brick (*stubbornly evasive*)   Believing . . .

Big Daddy   I don't know what the hell you mean by believing and I don't think you know what you mean by believing, but if you still got sports in your blood, go back to sports announcing and −

Brick   Sit in a glass box watching games I can't play? Describing what I can't do while players do it? Sweating out their disgust and confusion in contests I'm not fit for? Drinkin' a Coke, half bourbon, so I can stand it? That's no goddam good any more, no help – time just outran me, Big Daddy – got there first . . .

Big Daddy   I think you're passing the buck.

Brick   You know many drinkin' men?

Big Daddy (*with a slight, charming smile*)   I have known a fair number of that species.

Brick   Could any of them tell you why he drank?

Big Daddy   Yep, you're passin' the buck to things like time and disgust with 'mendacity' and – crap! – if you got to use that kind of language about a thing, it's ninety-proof bull, and I'm not buying any.

Brick   I had to give you a reason to get a drink!

Big Daddy   You started drinkin' when your friend Skipper died.

Silence for five beats. Then **Brick** *makes a startled movement, reaching for his crutch.*

Brick   What are you suggesting?

Big Daddy   I'm suggesting nothing.

The shuffle and clop of **Brick**'*s rapid hobble away from his father's steady, grave attention.*

Big Daddy   – But Gooper an' Mae suggested that there was something not right exactly in your –

Brick (*stopping short downstage as if backed to a wall*)   'Not right'?

Big Daddy   Not, well, exactly *normal* in your friendship with –

Brick   They suggested that, too? I thought that was Maggie's suggestion.

Brick's *detachment is at last broken through. His heart is accelerated; his forehead sweat-beaded; his breath becomes more rapid and his voice hoarse. The thing they're discussing, timidly and painfully on the side of* **Big Daddy**, *fiercely, violently on* **Brick**'s *side, is the inadmissible thing that Skipper died to disavow between them. The fact that if it existed it had to be disavowed to 'keep face' in the world they lived in, may be at the heart of the 'mendacity' that* **Brick** *drinks to kill his disgust with. It may be the root of his collapse. Or maybe it is only a single manifestation of it, not even the most important. The bird that I hope to catch in the net of this play is not the solution of one man's psychological problem. I'm trying to catch the true quality of experience in a group of people, that cloudy, flickering, evanescent — fiercely charged! — interplay of live human beings in the thundercloud of a common crisis. Some mystery should be left in the revelation of character in a play, just as a great deal of mystery is always left in the revelation of character in life, even in one's own character to himself. This does not absolve the playwright of his duty to observe and probe as clearly and deeply as he legitimately can: but it should steer him away from 'pat' conclusions, facile definitions which make a play just a play, not a snare for the truth of human experience.*

The following scene should be played with great concentration, with most of the power leashed but palpable in what is left unspoken.

Brick   Who else's suggestion is it, is it *yours*? How many others thought that Skipper and I were —

Big Daddy (*gently*)   Now, hold on, hold on a minute, son. — I knocked around in my time.

Brick   What's that got to do with —

Big Daddy   I said 'Hold on!' — I bummed, I bummed this country till I was —

Brick   Whose suggestion, who else's suggestion is it?

Big Daddy   Slept in hobo jungles and railroad Y's and flophouses in all cities before I —

Brick   Oh, *you* think so, too, you call me your son and a queer. Oh! Maybe that's why you put Maggie and me in this room that was Jack Straw's and Peter Ochello's, in which that pair of old sisters slept in a double bed where both of 'em died!

Big Daddy   *Now just don't go throwing rocks at –*

Suddenly **Reverend Tooker** *appears in the gallery doors, his head slightly, playfully, fatuously cocked, with a practised clergyman's smile, sincere as a bird call blown on a hunter's whistle, the living embodiment of the pious, conventional lie.*

Big Daddy *gasps a little at this perfectly timed, but incongruous, apparition.*

Big Daddy   – What're you lookin' for, Preacher?

Reverend Tooker   The gentleman's lavatory, ha ha! – heh, heh . . .

Big Daddy (*with strained courtesy*)   – Go back out and walk down to the other end of the gallery, Reverend Tooker, and use the bathroom connected with my bedroom, and if you can't find it, ask them where it is!

Reverend Tooker   Ah, thanks.

He goes out with a deprecatory chuckle.

Big Daddy   It's hard to talk in this place . . .

Brick   Son of a – !

Big Daddy (*leaving a lot unspoken*)   – I seen all things and understood a lot of them, till 1910. Christ, the year that – I had worn my shoes through, hocked my – I hopped on a yellow dog freight car half a mile down the road, slept in a wagon of cotton outside the gin – Jack Straw an' Peter Ochello took me in. Hired me to manage this place which grew into this one. – When Jack Straw died – why, old Peter Ochello quit eatin' like a dog does when its master's dead, and died, too!

Brick   Christ!

Big Daddy   I'm just saying I understand such –

Brick (*violently*)   Skipper is dead. I have not quit eating!

Big Daddy   No, but you started drinking.

Brick *wheels on his crutch and hurls his glass across the room shouting.*

Brick   YOU THINK SO, TOO?

Footsteps run on the gallery. There are women's calls.

Big Daddy *goes toward the door.*

Brick *is transformed, as if a quiet mountain blew suddenly up in volcanic flame.*

Brick   You think so, too? You think so, too? You think me an' Skipper did, did, did! – *sodomy!* – together?

Big Daddy   Hold – !

Brick   That what you –

Big Daddy   – *ON* – a minute!

Brick   You think we did dirty things between us, Skipper an' –

Big Daddy   Why are you shouting like that? Why are you –

Brick   – Me, is that what you think of Skipper, is that –

Big Daddy   – so excited? I don't think nothing. I don't know nothing. I'm simply telling you what –

Brick   You think that Skipper and me were a pair of dirty old men?

Big Daddy   Now that's –

Brick   Straw? Ochello? A couple of –

Big Daddy   Now just –

Brick   – fucking sissies? Queers? Is that what you –

Big Daddy   Shhh.

Brick   – think?

He loses his balance and pitches to his knees without noticing the pain. He grabs the bed and drags himself up.

Big Daddy Jesus! – Whew . . . Grab my hand!

Brick Naw, I don't want your hand . . .

Big Daddy Well, I want yours. Git up!

He draws him up, keeps an arm about him with concern and affection.

You broken out in a sweat! You're panting like you'd run a race with –

Brick (*freeing himself from his father's hold*) Big Daddy, you shock me, Big Daddy, you, you – *shock* me! Talkin' so –

He turns away from his father.

– casually! – about a – thing like that . . .

– Don't you know how people *feel* about things like that? How, how *disgusted* they are by things like that? Why, at Ole Miss when it was discovered a pledge to our fraternity, Skipper's and mine, did a, *attempted* to do a, unnatural thing with –

We not only dropped him like a hot rock! – We told him to git off the campus, and he did, he got! – All the way to –

He halts, breathless.

Big Daddy – Where?

Brick – North Africa, last I heard!

Big Daddy Well, I have come back from further away than that, I have just now returned from the other side of the moon, death's country, son, and I'm not easy to shock by anything here.

He comes downstage and faces out.

Always, anyhow, lived with too much space around me to be infected by ideas of other people. One thing you can grow on a big place more important than cotton! – is *tolerance*! – I grown it.

He returns toward **Brick**.

Brick   Why can't exceptional friendship, *real, real, deep, deep friendship!* between two men be respected as something clean and decent without being thought of as –

Big Daddy   It can, it is, for God's sake.

Brick   – *Fairies* . . .

In his utterance of this word, we gauge the wide and profound reach of the conventional mores he got from the world that crowned him with early laurel.

Big Daddy   I told Mae an' Gooper –

Brick   Frig Mae and Gooper, frig all dirty lies and liars! – Skipper and me had a clean, true thing between us! – had a clean friendship, practically all our lives, till Maggie got the idea you're talking about. Normal? No! – It was too rare to be normal, any true thing between two people is too rare to be normal. Oh, once in a while he put his hand on my shoulder or I'd put mine on his, oh, maybe even, when we were touring the country in pro-football an' shared hotel-rooms we'd reach across the space between the two beds and shake hands to say goodnight, yeah, one or two times we –

Big Daddy   Brick, nobody thinks that that's not normal!

Brick   Well, they're mistaken, it was! It was a pure an' true thing an' that's not normal.

Mae (*off stage*)   Big Daddy, they're startin' the fireworks.

They both stare straight at each other for a long moment. The tension breaks and both turn away as if tired.

Big Daddy   Yeah, it's – hard t' – talk . . .

Brick   All right, then, let's – let it go . . .

Big Daddy   Why did Skipper crack up? Why have you?

Brick *looks back at his father again. He has already decided, without knowing that he has made this decision, that he is going to tell his father* *that he is dying of cancer. Only this could even the score between them: one inadmissible thing in return for another.*

Brick (*ominously*)   All right. You're asking for it, Big Daddy. We're finally going to have that real true talk you wanted. It's too late to stop it, now, we got to carry it through and cover every subject.

He hobbles back to the liquor cabinet.

Uh-huh.

He opens the ice bucket and picks up the silver tongs with slow admiration of their frosty brightness.

Maggie declares that Skipper and I went into pro-football after we left 'Ole Miss' because we were scared to grow up . . .

He moves downstage with the shuffle and clop of a cripple on a crutch. As **Margaret** *did when her speech became 'recitative', he looks out into the house, commanding its attention by his direct, concentrated gaze – a broken, 'tragically elegant' figure telling simply as much as he knows of 'the Truth':*

– Wanted to – keep on tossing – those long, long! – high, high! – passes that – couldn't be intercepted except by time, the aerial attack that made us famous! And so we did, we did, we kept it up for one season, that aerial attack, we held it high! – Yeah, but –

– that summer, Maggie, she laid the law down to me, said, Now or never, and so I married Maggie . . .

Big Daddy   How was Maggie in bed?

Brick (*wryly*)   Great! the greatest!

Big Daddy *nods as if he thought so.*

Brick   She went on the road that fall with the Dixie Stars. Oh, she made a great show of being the world's best sport. She wore a – wore a – tall bearskin cap! A shako, they call it, a dyed moleskin coat, a moleskin coat dyed red! – Cut up crazy! Rented hotel ballrooms for victory celebrations, wouldn't cancel them when it – turned out – defeat . . .

MAGGIE THE CAT! Ha ha!

Big Daddy *nods.*

Brick   – But Skipper, he had some fever which came back on him which doctors couldn't explain and I got that injury – turned out to be just a shadow on the X-ray plate – and a touch of bursitis . . .

I lay in a hospital bed, watched our games on TV, saw Maggie on the bench next to Skipper when he was hauled out of a game for stumbles, fumbles! – Burned me up the way she hung on his arm! – Y'know, I think that Maggie had always felt sort of left out because she and me never got any closer together than two people just get in bed, which is not much closer than two cats on a – fence humping . . .

So! She took this time to work on poor dumb Skipper. He was a less than average student at Ole Miss, you know that, don't you?! – Poured in his mind the dirty, false idea that what we were, him and me, was a frustrated case of that ole pair of sisters that lived in this room, Jack Straw and Peter Ochello! – He, poor Skipper, went to bed with Maggie to prove it wasn't true, and when it didn't work out, he thought it *was* true! – Skipper broke in two like a rotten stick – nobody ever turned so fast to a lush – or died of it so quick . . .

– Now are you satisfied?

Big Daddy *has listened to this story, dividing the grain from the chaff. Now he looks at his son.*

Big Daddy   Are *you* satisfied?

Brick   With what?

Big Daddy   That half-ass story!

Brick   What's half-ass about it?

Big Daddy   Something's left out of that story. What did you leave out?

The phone has started ringing in the hall.

Gooper (*off stage*)   Hello.

As if it reminded him of something, **Brick** *glances suddenly toward the sound and says:*

Brick   Yes! – I left out a long-distance call which I had from Skipper –

Gooper   Speaking, go ahead.

Brick   – In which he made a drunken confession to me and on which I hung up!

Gooper   No.

Brick   – Last time we spoke to each other in our lives . . .

Gooper   No, sir.

Big Daddy   You musta said something to him before you hung up.

Brick   What could I say to him?

Big Daddy   Anything. Something.

Brick   Nothing.

Big Daddy   Just hung up?

Brick   Just hung up.

Big Daddy   Uh-huh. Anyhow now! – we have tracked down the lie with which you're disgusted and which you are drinking to kill your disgust with, Brick. You been passing the buck. This disgust with mendacity is disgust with yourself.

You! – dug the grave of your friend and kicked him in it! – before you'd face truth with him!

Brick   *His* truth, not *mine*!

Big Daddy   His truth, okay! But you wouldn't face it with him!

Brick   Who *can* face truth? Can *you*?

Big Daddy   Now don't start passin' the rotten buck again, boy!

Brick   How about these birthday congratulations, these many, many happy returns of the day, when ev'rybody knows there won't be any except you!

Gooper, *who has answered the hall phone, lets out a high, shrill laugh; the voice becomes audible saying: 'No, no, you got it all wrong! Upside down! Are you crazy?'*

Brick *suddenly catches his breath as he realises that he has made a shocking disclosure. He hobbles a few paces, then freezes, and without looking at his father's shocked face, says:*

Brick   Let's, let's – go out, now, and – watch the fireworks. Come on, Big Daddy.

Big Daddy *moves suddenly forward and grabs hold of the boy's crutch like it was a weapon for which they were fighting for possession.*

Big Daddy   Oh, no, no! No one's going out! What did you start to say?

Brick   I don't remember.

Big Daddy   'Many happy returns when they know there won't be any'?

Brick   Aw, hell, Big Daddy, forget it. Come on out on the gallery and look at the fireworks they're shooting off for your birthday . . .

Big Daddy   First you finish that remark you were makin' before you cut off. 'Many happy returns when they know there won't be any'? – Ain't that what you just said?

Brick   Look, now. I can get around without that crutch if I have to but it would be a lot easier on the furniture an' glassware if I didn' have to go swinging along like Tarzan of th' –

Big Daddy   FINISH! WHAT YOU WAS SAYIN'!

An eerie green glow shows in sky behind him.

Brick (*sucking the ice in his glass, speech becoming thick*)   Leave th' place to Gooper and Mae an' their five little same little monkeys. All I want is –

Big Daddy   'LEAVE TH' PLACE', did you say?

Brick (*vaguely*)   All twenty-eight thousand acres of the richest land this side of the valley Nile.

Big Daddy   Who said I was 'leaving the place' to Gooper or anybody? This is my sixty-fifth birthday! I got fifteen years or twenty years left in me! I'll outlive *you*! I'll bury you an' have to pay for your coffin!

Brick   Sure. Many happy returns. Now let's go watch the fireworks, come on, let's –

Big Daddy   Lying, have they been lying? About the report from th' clinic? Did they, did they – find something? – *Cancer.* Maybe?

Brick   Mendacity is a system that we live in. Liquor is one way out an' death's the other . . .

He takes the crutch from **Big Daddy***'s loose grip and swings out on the gallery leaving the doors open.*

A song, 'Pick a Bale of Cotton', is heard.

Mae (*appearing in door*)   Oh, Big Daddy, the field hands are singin' to' you!

Brick   I'm sorry, Big Daddy. My head don't work any more and it's hard for me to understand how anybody could care if he lived or died or was dying or cared about anything but whether or not there was liquor left in the bottle and so I said what I said without thinking. In some ways I'm no better than the others, in some ways worse because I'm less alive. Maybe it's being alive that makes them lie, and being almost *not* alive makes me sort of accidentally truthful – I don't know but – anyway – we've been friends . . .

– And being friends is telling each other the truth . . .

There is a pause.

You told *me*! I told *you*!

Big Daddy (*slowly and passionately*)   CHRIST – DAMN –

Gooper (*off stage*)   Let her go!

Fireworks off stage right.

Big Daddy   – ALL – LYING SONS OF – LYING BITCHES!

He straightens at last and crosses to the inside door. At the door he turns and looks back as if he had some desperate question he couldn't put into words. Then he nods reflectively and says in a hoarse voice:

Yes, all liars, all liars, all lying dying liars!

This is said slowly, slowly, with a fierce revulsion. He goes on out.

– Lying! Dying! Liars!

Brick *remains motionless as the lights dim out and the curtain falls.*

Curtain.

Act Three

There is no lapse of time. **Big Daddy** *is seen leaving as at the end of Act Two.*

Big Daddy ALL LYIN' – DYIN'! – LIARS! LIARS! – LIARS!

Margaret *enters.*

Margaret Brick, what in the name of God was goin' on in this room?

Dixie *and* **Trixie** *enter through the doors and circle around* **Margaret** *shouting.* **Mae** *enters from the lower gallery window.*

Mae Dixie, Trixie, you quit that!

Gooper *enters through the doors.*

Mae Gooper, will y' please get these kiddies to bed right now!

Gooper Mae, you seen Big Mama?

Mae Not yet.

Gooper *and kids exit through the doors.* **Reverend Tooker** *enters through the windows.*

Reverend Tooker Those kiddies are so full of vitality. I think I'll have to be starting back to town.

Mae Not yet, Preacher. You know we regard you as a member of this family, one of our closest an' dearest, so you just got t' be with us when Doc Baugh gives Big Mama th' actual truth about th' report from the clinic.

Margaret Where do you think you're going?

Brick Out for some air.

Margaret Why'd Big Daddy shout 'Liars'?

Mae Has Big Daddy gone to bed, Brick?

Gooper (*entering*) Now where is that old lady?

Reverend Tooker   I'll look for her.

He exits to the gallery.

Mae   Cain'tcha find her, Gooper?

Gooper   She's avoidin' this talk.

Mae   I think she senses somethin'.

Margaret (*going out on the gallery to* **Brick**)   Brick, they're goin' to tell Big Mama the truth about Big Daddy and she's goin' to need you.

Doctor Baugh   This is going to be painful.

Mae   Painful things caint always be avoided.

Reverend Tooker   I see Big Mama.

Gooper   Hey, Big Mama, come here.

Mae   Hush, Gooper, don't holler.

Big Mama (*entering*)   Too much smell of burnt fireworks makes me feel a little bit sick at my stomach. – Where is Big Daddy?

Mae   That's what I want to know, where has Big Daddy gone?

Big Mama   He must have turned in, I reckon he went to baid . . .

Gooper   Well, then, now we can talk.

Big Mama   What *is* this talk, *what* talk?

Margaret *appears on the gallery, talking to* **Doctor Baugh**.

Margaret (*musically*)   My family freed their slaves ten years before abolition. My great-great-grandfather gave his slaves their freedom five years before the War between the States started!

Mae   Oh, for God's sake! Maggie's climbed back up in her family tree!

Margaret (*sweetly*)   What, Mae?

The pace must be very quick: great Southern animation.

Big Mama (*addressing them all*)   I think Big Daddy was just worn out. He loves his family, he loves to have them around him, but it's a strain on his nerves. He wasn't himself tonight, Big Daddy wasn't himself, I could tell he was all worked up.

Reverend Tooker   I think he's remarkable.

Big Mama   Yaisss! Just remarkable. Did you all notice the food he ate at that table? Did you all notice the supper he put away? Why he ate like a hawss!

Gooper   I hope he doesn't regret it.

Big Mama   What? Why that man – ate a huge piece of cawn bread with molasses on it! Helped himself twice to hoppin' John.

Margaret   Big Daddy loves hoppin' John. – We had a real country dinner.

Big Mama (*overlapping* **Margaret**)   Yaiss, he simply adores it! an' candied yams? Son? That man put away enough food at that table to stuff a *field* hand!

Gooper (*with grim relish*)   I hope he don't have to pay for it later on . . .

Big Mama (*fiercely*)   What's *that*, Gooper?

Mae   Gooper says he hopes Big Daddy doesn't suffer tonight.

Big Mama   Oh, shoot, Gooper says, Gooper says! Why should Big Daddy suffer for satisfying a normal appetite? There's nothin' wrong with that man but nerves, he's sound as a dollar! And now he knows he is an' that's why he ate such a supper. He had a big load off his mind, knowin' he wasn't doomed t' – what he thought he was doomed to . . .

Margaret (*sadly and sweetly*)   Bless his old sweet soul . . .

Big Mama (*vaguely*)   Yais, bless his heart, where's Brick?

Mae   Outside.

Gooper   Drinkin' . . .

Big Mama   I know he's drinkin'. Cain't I see he's drinkin' without you continually tellin' me that boy's drinkin'?

Margaret   Good for you, Big Mama!

She applauds.

Big Mama   Other people *drink* and *have* drunk an' will *drink*, as long as they make that stuff an' put it in bottles.

Margaret   That's the truth. I never trusted a man that didn't drink.

Big Mama   *Brick? Brick!*

Margaret   He's still on the gall'ry. I'll go bring him in so we can talk.

Big Mama (*worriedly*)   I don't know what this mysterious family conference is about.

Awkward silence. **Big Mama** *looks from face to face, then belches slightly and mutters, 'Excuse me . . . ' She opens an ornamental fan suspended about her throat. A black lace fan to go with her black lace gown, and fans her wilting corsage, sniffing nervously and looking from face to face in the uncomfortable silence as* **Margaret** *calls 'Brick?' and* **Brick** *sings to the moon on the gallery.*

Margaret   Brick, they're gonna tell Big Mama the truth an' she's gonna need you.

Big Mama   I don't know what's wrong here, you all have such long faces! Open that door on the hall and let some air circulate through here, will you please, Gooper?

Mae   I think we'd better leave that door closed, Big Mama, till after the talk.

Margaret   Brick!

Big Mama   Reveren' Tooker, will *you* please open that door?

Reverend Tooker   I sure will, Big Mama.

Mae   I just didn't think we ought t' take any chance of Big Daddy hearin' a word of this discussion.

Big Mama   *I swan!* Nothing's going to be said in Big Daddy's house that he caint hear if he want to!

Gooper   Well, Big Mama, it's –

Mae *gives him a quick, hard poke to shut him up. He glares at her fiercely as she circles before him like a burlesque ballerina, raising her skinny bare arms over her head, jangling her bracelets, exclaiming:*

Mae   *A breeze! A breeze!*

Reverend Tooker   I think this house is the coolest house in the Delta. – Did you all know that Halsey Banks's widow put air-conditioning units in the church and rectory at Friar's Point in memory of Halsey?

General conversation has resumed; everybody is chatting so that the stage sounds like a bird cage.

Gooper   Too bad nobody cools your church off for you. I bet you sweat in that pulpit these hot Sundays, Reverend Tooker.

Reverend Tooker   Yes, my vestments are drenched. Last Sunday the gold in my chasuble faded into the purple.

Gooper   Reveren', you musta been preachin' hell's fire last Sunday.

Mae (*at the same time to* **Doctor Baugh**)   You reckon those vitamin B12 injections are what they're cracked up t' be, Doc Baugh?

Doctor Baugh   Well, if you want to be stuck with something I guess they're as good to be stuck with as anything else.

Big Mama (*at the gallery door*)   *Maggie, Maggie, aren't you comin' with Brick?*

Mae (*suddenly and loudly, creating a silence*)   *I have a strange feeling, I have a peculiar feeling!*

Big Mama (*turning from the gallery*)   What feeling?

Mae   That Brick said somethin' he shouldn't of said t' Big Daddy.

Big Mama   Now what on earth could Brick of said t' Big Daddy that he shouldn't say?

Gooper   Big Mama, there's somethin' –

Mae   NOW, WAIT!

She rushes up to **Big Mama** *and gives her a quick hug and kiss.* **Big Mama** *pushes her impatiently off.*

Doctor Baugh   In my day they had what they call the Keeley cure for heavy drinkers.

Big Mama   Shoot!

Doctor Baugh   But now I understand they just take some kind of tablets.

Gooper   They call them 'Annie Bust' tablets.

Big Mama   *Brick* don't need to take *nothin'*.

Brick *and* **Margaret** *appear in gallery doors,* **Big Mama** *unaware of his presence behind her.*

Big Mama   That boy is just broken up over Skipper's death. You know how poor Skipper died. They gave him a big, big dose of that sodium amytal stuff at his home and then they called the ambulance and give him another big, big dose of it at the hospital and that and all of the alcohol in his system fa' months an' months just proved too much for his heart . . . I'm scared of needles! I'm more scared of a needle than the knife . . . I think more people have been needled out of this world than –

She stops short and wheels about.

Oh – here's Brick! My precious baby –

She turns upon **Brick** *with short, fat arms extended, at the same time uttering a loud, short sob, which is both comic and touching.* **Brick** *smiles and bows slightly, making a burlesque gesture of gallantry for* **Margaret** *to pass before him into the room. Then he hobbles on his* *crutch directly to the liquor cabinet and there is absolute silence, with everybody looking at* **Brick** *as everybody has always looked at* **Brick** *when he spoke or moved or appeared. One by one he drops ice cubes in his glass, then suddenly, but not quickly, looks back over his shoulder with a wry, charming smile, and says:*

Brick   I'm sorry! Anyone else?

Big Mama (*sadly*)   No, son. I *wish* you wouldn't!

Brick   I wish I didn't have to, Big Mama, but I'm still waiting for that click in my head which makes it all smooth out!

Big Mama   Ow, Brick, you – BREAK MY HEART!

Margaret (*at same time*)   *Brick, go sit with Big Mama!*

Big Mama   I just cain't staiiiiii-nnnnnnnd-it . . .

She sobs.

Mae   Now that we're all assembled –

Gooper   We kin talk . . .

Big Mama   Breaks my heart . . .

Margaret   Sit with Big Mama, Brick, and hold her hand.

Big Mama *sniffs very loudly three times, almost like three drumbeats in the pocket of silence.*

Brick   You do that, Maggie. I'm a restless cripple. I got to stay on my crutch.

Brick *hobbles to the gallery door; leans there as if waiting.*

Mae *sits beside* **Big Mama**, *while* **Gooper** *moves in front and sits on the end of the couch, facing her.* **Reverend Tooker** *moves nervously into the space between them; on the other side,* **Doctor Baugh** *stands looking at nothing in particular and lights a cigar.* **Margaret** *turns away.*

Big Mama   Why're you all *surroundin'* me – like this? Why're you all starin' at me like this an' makin' signs at each other?

Reverend Tooker *steps back startled.*

Mae   Calm yourself, Big Mama.

Big Mama   Calm you'self, *you'self*, Sister Woman. How could I calm myself with everyone starin' at me as if big drops of blood had broken out on m'face? What's this all about, annh! What?

Gooper *coughs and takes a center position.*

Gooper   Now, Doc Baugh.

Mae   Doc Baugh?

Gooper   Big Mama wants to know the complete truth about the report we got from the Ochsner Clinic.

Mae (*eagerly*)   – on Big Daddy's condition!

Gooper   Yais, on Big Daddy's condition, we got to face it.

Doctor Baugh   Well . . .

Big Mama (*terrified, rising*)   Is there? Something? Something that I? Don't – know?

In these few words, this startled, very soft, question, **Big Mama** *reviews the history of her forty-five years with* **Big Daddy**, *her great, almost embarrassingly true-hearted and simple-minded devotion to* **Big Daddy**, *who must have had something* **Brick** *has, who made himself loved so much by the 'simple expedient' of not loving enough to disturb his charming detachment, also once coupled, like* **Brick**, *with virile beauty.*

Big Mama *has a dignity at this moment; she almost stops being fat.*

Doctor Baugh (*after a pause, uncomfortably*)   Yes? – Well –

Big Mama   I!!! – want to – *knowwwwww* . . .

Immediately she thrusts her fist to her mouth as if to deny that statement. Then for some curious reason, she snatches the withered corsage from her breast and hurls it on the floor and steps on it with her short, fat feet.

Somebody must be lyin'! – I want to know!

Mae   Sit down, Big Mama, sit down on this sofa.

Margaret   Brick, go sit with Big Mama.

Big Mama   *What is it, what is it?*

Doctor Baugh   I never have seen a more thorough examination than Big Daddy Pollitt was given in all my experience with the Ochsner Clinic.

Gooper   It's one of the best in the country.

Mae   It's THE best in the country – bar *none*!

For some reason she gives **Gooper** *a violent poke as she goes past him. He slaps at her hand without removing his eyes from his mother's face.*

Doctor Baugh   Of course they were ninety-nine and nine-tenths per cent sure before they even started.

Big Mama   Sure of what, sure of what, sure of – *what?* – *what?*

She catches her breath in a startled sob. **Mae** *kisses her quickly. She thrusts* **Mae** *fiercely away from her, staring at the* **Doctor**.

Mae   Mommy, be a brave girl!

Brick (*in the doorway, softly*)
  'By the light, by the light,
  Of the sil-ve-ry mo-oo-n . . . '

Gooper   Shut up! – Brick.

Brick   Sorry . . .

He wanders out on the gallery.

Doctor Baugh   But now, you see, Big Mama, they cut a piece off this growth, a specimen of the tissue and –

Big Mama   Growth? You told Big Daddy –

Doctor Baugh   Now wait.

Big Mama (*fiercely*)   You told me and Big Daddy there wasn't a thing wrong with him but –

Mae   Big Mama, they always –

Gooper   Let Doc Baugh talk, will yuh?

Big Mama   – little spastic condition of –

Her breath gives out in a sob.

Doctor Baugh   Yes, that's what we told Big Daddy. But we had this bit of tissue run through the laboratory and I'm sorry to say the test was positive on it. It's – well – malignant . . .

Pause.

Big Mama   – Cancer?! Cancer?!

Doctor Baugh *nods gravely.* **Big Mama** *gives a long gasping cry.*

Mae *and* **Gooper**   Now, now, now, Big Mama, you had to know . . .

Big Mama   WHY DIDN'T THEY CUT IT OUT OF HIM? HANH? HANH?

Doctor Baugh   Involved too much, Big Mama, too many organs affected.

Mae   Big Mama, the liver's affected and so's the kidneys, both! It's gone way past what they call a –

Gooper   A surgical risk.

Mae   – Uh-huh . . .

Big Mama *draws a breath like a dying gasp.*

Reverend Tooker   Tch, tch, tch, tch, tch!

Doctor Baugh   Yes it's gone past the knife.

Mae   *That's why he's turned yellow, Mommy!*

Big Mama   *Git away from me, git away from me, Mae!*

She rises abruptly.

I want Brick! Where's Brick? Where is my only son?

Mae   Mama! Did she say '*only* son'?

Gooper   What does that make *me*?

Mae   A sober responsible man with five precious children! – Six!

Big Mama   I want Brick to tell me! Brick! Brick!

Margaret (*rising from her reflections in a corner*)   Brick was so upset he went back out.

Big Mama   *Brick!*

Margaret   Mama, let *me* tell you!

Big Mama   No, no, leave me alone, you're not my blood!

Gooper   *Mama, I'm your son!* Listen to *me*!

Mae   Gooper's your son, he's your first-born!

Big Mama   Gooper never liked Daddy.

Mae (*as if terribly shocked*)   That's not TRUE!

There is a pause. The minister coughs and rises.

Reverend Tooker (*to* **Mae**)   I think I'd better slip away at this point.

Discreetly.

Good night, good night, everybody, and God bless you all . . . on this place . . .

He slips out.

Mae *coughs and points at* **Big Mama**.

Gooper   Well, Big Mama . . .

He sighs.

Big Mama   It's all a mistake, I know it's just a bad dream.

Doctor Baugh   We're gonna keep Big Daddy as comfortable as we can.

Big Mama   Yes, it's just a bad dream, that's all it is, it's just an awful dream.

Gooper   In my opinion Big Daddy is having some pain but won't admit that he has it.

Big Mama   Just a dream, a bad dream.

Doctor Baugh   That's what lots of them do, they think if they don't admit they're having the pain they can sort of escape the fact of it.

Gooper (*with relish*)   Yes, they get sly about it, they get real sly about it.

Mae   Gooper and I think –

Gooper   Shut up, Mae! Big Mama, I think – Big Daddy ought to be started on morphine.

Big Mama   Nobody's going to give Big Daddy morphine.

Doctor Baugh   Now, Big Mama, when that pain strikes it's going to strike mighty hard and Big Daddy's going to need the needle to bear it.

Big Mama   I tell you, nobody's going to give him morphine.

Mae   Big Mama, you don't want to see Big Daddy suffer, you know you –

Gooper, *standing beside her, gives her a savage poke.*

Doctor Baugh (*placing a package on the table*)   I'm leaving this stuff here, so if there's a sudden attack you all won't have to send out for it.

Mae   I know how to give a hypo.

Big Mama   Nobody's gonna give Big Daddy morphine.

Gooper   Mae took a course in nursing during the war.

Margaret   Somehow I don't think Big Daddy would want Mae to give him a hypo.

Mae   You think he'd want *you* to do it?

Doctor Baugh   Well . . .

He rises.

Gooper   Doctor Baugh is goin'.

Doctor Baugh   Yes, I got to be goin'. Well, keep your chin up, Big Mama.

Gooper (*with jocularity*)   She's gonna keep *both* chins up, aren't you, Big Mama?

Big Mama *sobs.*

Gooper   Now stop that, Big Mama.

(*At the door with* **Doctor Baugh**.) Well, Doc, we sure do appreciate all you done. I'm telling you, we're surely obligated to you for –

Doctor Baugh *has gone out without a glance at him.*

Gooper   – I guess that doctor has got a lot on his mind but it wouldn't hurt him to act a little more human . . .

Big Mama *sobs.*

Gooper   Now be a brave girl, Mommy.

Big Mama   It's not true, I know that it's just not true!

Gooper   Mama, those tests are infallible!

Big Mama   Why are you so determined to see your father daid?

Mae   Big Mama!

Margaret (*gently*)   I know what Big Mama means.

Mae (*fiercely*)   Oh, do you?

Margaret (*quietly and very sadly*)   Yes, I think I do.

Mae   For a newcomer in the family you sure do show a lot of understanding.

Margaret   Understanding is needed on this place.

Mae   I guess you must have needed a lot of it in your family, Maggie, with your father's liquor problem and now you've got Brick with his!

Margaret   Brick does not have a liquor problem at all. Brick is devoted to Big Daddy. This thing is a terrible strain on him.

Big Mama   Brick is Big Daddy's boy, but he drinks too much and it worries me and Big Daddy, and, Margaret, you've got to co-operate with us, you've got to co-operate with Big Daddy and me in getting Brick straightened out. Because it will break Big Daddy's heart if Brick don't pull himself together and take hold of things.

Mae   Take hold of *what* things, Big Mama?

Big Mama   The place.

There is a quick violent look between **Mae** *and* **Gooper**.

Gooper   Big Mama, you've had a shock.

Mae   Yais, we've all had a shock, but . . .

Gooper   Let's be realistic –

Mae   – Big Daddy would never, would *never*, be foolish enough to –

Gooper   – put this place in irresponsible hands!

Big Mama   Big Daddy ain't going to leave the place in anybody's hands; Big Daddy is *not* going to die. I want you to get that in your heads, all of you!

Mae   Mommy, Mommy, Big Mama, we're just as hopeful an' optimistic as you are about Big Daddy's prospects, we have faith in *prayer* – but nevertheless there are certain matters that have to be discussed an' dealt with, because otherwise –

Gooper   Eventualities have to be considered and now's the time . . . Mae, will you please get my brief case out of our room?

Mae   Yes, honey.

She rises and goes out through the hall door.

Gooper (*standing over* **Big Mama**)   Now, Big Mom. What you said just now was not at all true and you know it. I've always loved Big Daddy in my own quiet way. I never made a show of it, and I know that Big Daddy has always been fond of me in a quiet way, too, and he never made a show of it neither.

Mae *returns with* **Gooper**'s *brief case.*

Mae   Here's your brief case, Gooper, honey.

Gooper (*handing the brief case back to her*)   Thank you . . . Of cou'se, my relationship with Big Daddy is different from Brick's.

Mae   You're eight years older'n Brick an' always had t' carry a bigger load of th' responsibilities than Brick ever had t' carry. He never carried a thing in his life but a football or a highball.

Gooper   Mae, will y' let me talk, please?

Mae   Yes, honey.

Gooper   Now, a twenty-eight-thousand-acre plantation's a mighty big thing t' run.

Mae   Almost singlehanded.

Margaret *has gone out onto the gallery and can be heard calling softly to* **Brick**.

Big Mama   You never had to run this place! What are you talking about? As if Big Daddy was dead and in his grave, you had to run it? Why, you just helped him out with a few business details and had your law practice at the same time in Memphis!

Mae   Oh, Mommy, Mommy, Big Mommy! Let's be fair!

Margaret   Brick!

Mae   Why, Gooper has given himself body and soul to keeping this place up for the past five years since Big Daddy's health started failing.

Margaret   Brick!

Mae   Gooper won't say it, Gooper never thought of it as a duty, he just did it. And what did Brick do? Brick kept living in his past glory at college! Still a football player at twenty-seven!

Margaret (*returning alone*)   Who are you talking about now? Brick? A football player? He isn't a football player and you know it. Brick is a sports announcer on TV and one of the best-known ones in the country!

Mae   I'm talking about what he was.

Margaret   Well, I wish you would just stop talking about my husband.

Gooper   I've got a right to discuss my brother with other members of MY OWN family, which don't include *you*. Why don't you go out there and drink with Brick?

Margaret   I've never seen such malice toward a brother.

Gooper   How about his for me? Why, he can't stand to be in the same room with me!

Margaret   This is a deliberate campaign of vilification for the most disgusting and sordid reason on earth, and I know what it is! It's *avarice, avarice, greed, greed!*

Big Mama   *Oh, I'll scream! I will scream in a moment unless this stops!*

Gooper *has stalked up to* **Margaret** *with clenched fists at his sides as if he would strike her.* **Mae** *distorts her face again into a hideous grimace behind* **Margaret**'s *back.*

Big Mama (*sobs*)   Margaret. Child. Come here. Sit next to Big Mama.

Margaret   Precious Mommy. I'm sorry, I'm sorry, I – !

She bends her long graceful neck to press her forehead to **Big Mama**'s *bulging shoulder under its black chiffon.*

Mae   How beautiful, how touching, this display of devotion! Do you know why she's childless? She's childless because that big beautiful athlete husband of hers won't go to bed with her!

Gooper   You jest won't let me do this in a nice way, will yah? Aw right – I don't give a goddam if Big Daddy likes me or don't like me or did or never did or will or will never! I'm just appealing to a sense of common decency and fair play. I'll tell you the truth. I've resented Big Daddy's partiality to Brick ever since Brick was born, and the way I've been treated like I was just barely good enough to spit on and sometimes not even good enough for that. Big Daddy is dying of cancer, and it's spread all through him and it's attacked all his vital organs including the kidneys and right now he is sinking into uremia, and you all know what uremia is, it's poisoning of the whole system due to the failure of the body to eliminate its poisons.

Margaret (*to herself, downstage, hissingly*)   *Poisons, poisons! Venomous thoughts and words! In hearts and minds! —That's poisons!*

Gooper (*overlapping her*)   I am asking for a square deal, and, by God, I expect to get one. But if I don't get one, if there's any peculiar shenanigans going on around here behind my back, well, I'm not a corporation lawyer for nothing, I know how to protect my own interests.

Brick *enters from the gallery with a tranquil, blurred smile, carrying an empty glass with him.*

Brick   Storm coming up.

Gooper   Oh! A late arrival!

Mae   Behold the conquering hero comes!

Gooper   The — fabulous Brick Pollitt! Remember him? — Who could forget him!

Mae   He looks like he's been injured in a game!

Gooper   Yep, I'm afraid you'll have to warm the bench at the Sugar Bowl this year, Brick!

Mae *laughs shrilly.*

Gooper   Or was it the Rose Bowl that he made that famous run in?

Thunder.

Mae   The punch bowl, honey. It was in the punch bowl, the cut-glass punch bowl!

Gooper   Oh, that's right, I'm getting the bowls mixed up!

Margaret   Why don't you stop venting your malice and envy on a sick boy?

Big Mama   *Now you two hush, I mean it, hush, all of you, hush!*

Daisy *and* **Sookey**   Storm! Storm comin'! Storm! Storm!

Lacey   Brightie, close them shutters.

Gooper   Lacey, put the top up on my Cadillac, will yuh?

Lacey   Yes, suh, Mistah Pollitt!

Gooper (*at the same time*)   Big Mama, you know it's necessary for me t' go back to Memphis in th' mornin' t' represent the Parker estate in a lawsuit.

Mae *sits on the bed and arranges papers she has taken from the brief case.*

Big Mama   Is it, Gooper?

Mae   Yaiss.

Gooper   That's why I'm forced to – to bring up a problem that –

Mae   Somethin' that's too important t' be put off!

Gooper   If Brick was sober, he ought to be in on this.

Margaret   Brick is present; we're present.

Gooper   Well, good. I will now give you this outline my partner, Tom Bullitt, an' me have drawn up – a sort of dummy – trusteeship.

Margaret   Oh, that's it! You'll be in charge an' dole out remittances, will you?

Gooper   This we did as soon as we got the report on Big Daddy from th' Ochsner Laboratories. We did this thing, I mean we drew up this dummy outline with the advice and assistance of the Chairman of the Boa'd of Directors of th' Southern Plantahs Bank and Trust Company in Memphis,

C.C. Bellowes, a man who handles estates for all th' prominent fam'lies in West Tennessee and th' Delta.

Big Mama   Gooper?

Gooper (*crouching in front of* **Big Mama**)   Now this is not – not final, or anything like it. This is just a preliminary outline. But it does provide a basis – a design – a – possible, feasible – *plan*!

Margaret   Yes, I'll bet it's a plan.

Thunder.

Mae   It's a plan to protect the biggest estate in the Delta from irresponsibility an' –

Big Mama   Now you listen to me, all of you, you listen here! They's not goin' to be any more catty talk in my house! And Gooper, you put that away before I grab it out of your hand and tear it right up! I don't know what the hell's in it, and I don't want to know what the hell's in it. I'm talkin' in Big Daddy's language now; I'm his *wife*, not his *widow*, I'm still his *wife*! And I'm talkin' to you in his language an' –

Gooper   Big Mama, what I have here is –

Mae (*at the same time*)   Gooper explained that it's just a plan . . .

Big Mama   I don't care what you got there. Just put it back where it came from, an' don't let me see it again, not even the outside of the envelope of it! Is that understood? Basis! Plan! Preliminary! Design! I say – what is it Big Daddy always says when he's disgusted?.

Brick (*from the bar*)   Big Daddy says 'crap' when he's disgusted.

Big Mama (*rising*)   That's right – CRAP! I say CRAP too, like Big Daddy!

Thunder.

Mae   Coarse language doesn't seem called for in this –

Gooper   Somethin' in me is *deeply outraged* by hearin' you talk like this.

Big Mama   *Nobody's goin' to take nothin'!* – till Big Daddy lets go of it – maybe, just possibly, not – not even then! No, not even then!

Thunder.

Mae   Sookey, hurry up an' git that po'ch furniture covahed; want th' paint to come off?

Gooper   Lacey, put mah car away!

Lacey   Caint, Mistah Pollitt, you got the keys!

Gooper   Naw, you got 'em, man. Where th' keys to th' car, honey?

Mae   You got 'em in your pocket!

Brick
    'You can always hear me singin' this song,
    Show me the way to go home.'

Thunder distantly.

Big Mama   Brick! Come here, Brick, I need you. Tonight Brick looks like he used to look when he was a little boy, just like he did when he played wild games and used to come home when I hollered myself hoarse for him, all sweaty and pink-cheeked and sleepy, with his – red curls shining . . .

Brick *draws aside as he does from all physical contact and continues the song in a whisper, opening the ice bucket and dropping in the ice cubes one by one as if he were mixing some important chemical formula.*

Distant thunder.

Big Mama   Time goes by so fast. Nothin' can outrun it. Death commences too early – almost before you're half acquainted with life – you meet the other . . . Oh, you know we just got to love each other an' stay together, all of us, just as close as we can, especially now that such a *black* thing has come and moved into this place without invitation.

Awkwardly embracing **Brick**, *she presses her head to his shoulder.*

A dog howls off stage.

Oh, Brick, son of Big Daddy, Big Daddy does so love you. Y'know what would be his fondest dream come true? If before he passed on, if Big Daddy has to pass on . . .

A dog howls.

. . . you give him a child of yours, a grandson as much like his son as his son is like Big Daddy . . .

Margaret   I know that's Big Daddy's dream.

Big Mama   That's his dream.

Mae   Such a pity that Maggie and Brick can't oblige.

Big Daddy (*off down stage right on the gallery*)   Looks like the wind was takin' liberties with this place.

Servant (*off stage*)   Yes, sir, Mr Pollitt.

Margaret (*crossing to the right door*)   Big Daddy's on the gall'ry.

Big Mama *has turned toward the hall door at the sound of* **Big Daddy**'s *voice on the gallery.*

Big Mama   I can't stay here. He'll see somethin' in my eyes.

Big Daddy *enters the room from up stage right.*

Big Daddy   Can I come in?

He puts his cigar in an ash tray.

Margaret   Did the storm wake you up, Big Daddy?

Big Daddy   Which stawm are you talkin' about – th' one outside or th' hullballoo in here?

Gooper *squeezes past* **Big Daddy**.

Gooper   'Scuse me.

Mae *tries to squeeze past* **Big Daddy** *to join* **Gooper**, *but* **Big Daddy** *puts his arm firmly around her.*

Big Daddy   I heard some mighty loud talk. Sounded like somethin' important was bein' discussed. What was the pow-wow about?

Mae (*flustered*)   Why − nothin', Big Daddy . . .

Big Daddy (*crossing to extreme left center, taking* **Mae** *with him*)
What is that pregnant-lookin' envelope you're puttin' back in
your brief case, Gooper?

Gooper (*at the foot of the bed, caught, as he stuffs papers into envelope*)
That? Nothin',' suh − nothin' much of anythin' at all . . .

Big Daddy   Nothin'? It looks like a whole lot of nothin'!

He turns up stage to the group.

You all know th' story about th' young married couple −

Gooper   Yes, sir!

Big Daddy   Hello, Brick −

Brick   Hello, Big Daddy.

The group is arranged in a semicircle above **Big Daddy**, **Margaret**
at the extreme right, then **Mae** *and* **Gooper**, *then* **Big Mama**, *with*
Brick *at the left.*

Big Daddy   Young married couple took Junior out to th' zoo
one Sunday, inspected all of God's creatures in their cages,
with satisfaction.

Gooper   Satisfaction.

Big Daddy (*crossing to up stage center, facing front*)   This
afternoon was a warm afternoon in spring an' that ole elephant
had somethin' else on his mind which was bigger'n peanuts.
You know this story, Brick?

Gooper *nods.*

Brick   No, sir, I don't know it.

Big Daddy   Y'see, in th' cage adjoinin' they was a young
female elephant in heat!

Big Mama (*at* **Big Daddy**'*s shoulder*)   Oh, Big Daddy!

Big Daddy   What's the matter, preacher's gone, ain't he? All
right. That female elephant in the next cage was permeatin'

the atmosphere about her with a powerful and excitin' odor of female fertility! Huh! Ain't that a nice way to put it, Brick?

Brick   Yes, sir, nothin' wrong with it.

Big Daddy   Brick says th's nothin' wrong with it!

Big Mama   Oh, Big Daddy!

Big Daddy (*crossing to down stage center*)   So this ole bull elephant still had a couple of fornications left in him. He reared back his trunk an' got a whiff of that elephant lady next door! – began to paw at the dirt in his cage an' butt his head against the separatin' partition and, first thing y'know, there was a conspicuous change in his *profile* – very *conspicuous*! Ain't I tellin' this story in decent language, Brick?

Brick   Yes, sir, too fuckin' decent!

Big Daddy   So, the little boy pointed at it and said, 'What's that?' His mama said, 'Oh, that's-nothin'!' – His papa said, 'She's spoiled!'

Big Daddy crosses to **Brick** at left.

Big Daddy   You didn't laugh at that story, Brick.

Big Mama crosses to down stage right crying. **Margaret** goes to her. **Mae** and **Gooper** hold up stage right center.

Brick   No, sir, I didn't laugh at that story.

Big Daddy   What is the smell in this room? Don't you notice it, Brick? Don't you notice a powerful and obnoxious odor of mendacity in this room?

Brick   Yes, sir, I think I do, sir.

Gooper   Mae, Mae . . .

Big Daddy   There is nothing more powerful. Is there, Brick?

Brick   No, sir. No, sir, there isn't, an' nothin' more obnoxious.

Big Daddy   Brick agrees with me. The odor of mendacity is a powerful and obnoxious odor an' the stawm hasn't blown it away from this room yet. You notice it, Gooper?

Gooper   What, sir?

Big Daddy   How about you, Sister Woman? You notice the unpleasant odor of mendacity in this room?

Mae   Why, Big Daddy, I don't even know what that is.

Big Daddy   You can smell it. Hell it smells like death!

Big Mama *sobs.* **Big Daddy** *looks toward her.*

Big Daddy   What's wrong with that fat woman over there, loaded with diamonds? Hey, what's-you-name, what's the matter with you?

Margaret (*crossing toward* **Big Daddy**)   She had a slight dizzy spell, Big Daddy.

Big Daddy   You better watch that, Big Mama. A stroke is a bad way to go.

Margaret (*crossing to* **Big Daddy** *at center*)   Oh, Brick, Big Daddy has on your birthday present to him, Brick, he has on your cashmere robe, the softest material I have ever felt.

Big Daddy   Yeah, this is my soft birthday, Maggie . . . Not my gold or my silver birthday, but my soft birthday, everything's got to be soft for Big Daddy on this soft birthday.

Margaret *kneels before* **Big Daddy** *at center.*

Margaret   Big Daddy's got on his Chinese slippers that I gave him, Brick. Big Daddy, I haven't given you my big present yet, but now I will, now's the time for me to present it to you! I have an announcement to make!

Mae   What? What kind of announcement?

Gooper   A sports announcement, Maggie?

Margaret   Announcement of life beginning! A child is coming, sired by Brick, and out of Maggie the Cat! I have Brick's child in my body, an' that's my birthday present to Big Daddy on this birthday!

Big Daddy *looks at* **Brick** *who crosses behind* **Big Daddy** *to down stage portal, left.*

Big Daddy   Get up, girl, get up off your knees, girl.

He helps **Margaret** *to rise. He crosses above her, to her right, bites off the end of a fresh cigar, taken from his bathrobe pocket, as he studies* **Margaret**.

Big Daddy   *Uh-huh, this girl has life in her body, that's no lie!*

Big Mama   BIG DADDY'S DREAM COME TRUE!

Brick   JESUS!

Big Daddy (*crossing right below wicker stand*)   Gooper, I want my lawyer in the mornin'.

Brick   Where are you goin', Big Daddy?

Big Daddy   Son, I'm goin' up on the roof, to the belvedere on th' roof to look over my kingdom before I give up my kingdom – twenty-eight thousand acres of th' richest land this side of the valley Nile!

He exits through right doors, and down right on the gallery.

Big Mama (*following*)   Sweetheart, sweetheart, sweetheart – can I come with you?

She exits down stage right.

Margaret *is down stage center in the mirror area.* **Mae** *has joined* **Gooper** *and she gives him a fierce poke, making a low hissing sound and a grimace of fury.*

Gooper (*pushing her aside*)   Brick, could you possibly spare me one small shot of that liquor?

Brick   Why, help yourself, Gooper boy.

Gooper   I will.

Mae (*shrilly*)   Of course we know that this is – a lie.

Gooper   *Be still, Mae.*

Mae   I won't be still! I know she's made this up!

Gooper   Goddam it, I said shut up!

Margaret   Gracious! I didn't know that my little announcement was going to provoke such a storm!

Mae   *That* woman isn't *pregnant*!

Gooper   Who said she was?

Mae   *She* did.

Gooper   The doctor didn't. Doc Baugh didn't.

Margaret   I haven't gone to Doc Baugh.

Gooper   Then who'd you go to, Maggie?

Margaret   One of the best gynecologists in the South.

Gooper   Uh huh, uh huh! – I see . . .

He takes out a pencil and notebook.

May we have his name, please?

Margaret   No, you may not, Mister Prosecuting Attorney!

Mae   He doesn't have any name, he doesn't exist!

Margaret   Oh, he exists all right, and so does my child, Brick's baby!

Mae   You can't conceive a child by a man that won't sleep with you unless you think you're –

Brick *has turned on the phonograph. A scat song cuts* **Mae**'s *speech.*

Gooper   *Turn that off!*

Mae   We know it's a lie because we hear you in here; he won't sleep with you, we hear you! So don't imagine you're going to put a trick over on us, to fool a dying man with a –

A long drawn cry of agony and rage fills the house. **Margaret** *turns the phonograph down to a whisper. The cry is repeated.*

Mae   Did you hear that, Gooper, did you hear that?

Gooper   Sounds like the pain has struck.

Gooper   Come along and leave these lovebirds together in their nest!

He goes out first. **Mae** *follows but turns at the door, contorting her face and hissing at* **Margaret**.

Mae   *Liar!*

She slams the door.

Margaret *exhales with relief and moves a little unsteadily to catch hold of* **Brick**'s *arm.*

Margaret   Thank you for – keeping still . . .

Brick   OK, Maggie.

Margaret   It was gallant of you to save my face!

He now pours down three shots in quick succession and stands waiting, silent. All at once he turns with a smile and says:

Brick   *There!*

Margaret   What?

Brick   The *click* . . .

His gratitude seems almost infinite as he hobbles out on the gallery with a drink. We hear his crutch as he swings out of sight. Then, at some distance, he begins singing to himself a peaceful song. **Margaret** *holds the big pillow forlornly as if it were her only companion, for a few moments, then throws it on the bed. She rushes to the liquor cabinet, gathers all the bottles in her arms, turns about undecidedly, then runs out of the room with them, leaving the door ajar on the dim yellow hall.* **Brick** *is heard hobbling back along the gallery, singing his peaceful song. He comes back in, sees the pillow on the bed, laughs lightly, sadly, picks it up. He has it under his arm as* **Margaret** *returns to the room.* **Margaret** *softly shuts the door and leans against it, smiling softly at* **Brick**.

Margaret   Brick, I used to think that you were stronger than me and I didn't want to be overpowered by you. But now, since you've taken to liquor – you know what? – I guess it's bad, but now I'm stronger than you and I can love you more

truly! Don't move that pillow. I'll move it right back if you do!
– Brick?

She turns out all the lamps but a single rose-silk-shaded one by the bed.

I really have been to a doctor and I know what to do and –
Brick? – this is my time by the calendar to conceive?

Brick   Yes, I understand, Maggie. But how are you going to
conceive a child by a man in love with his liquor?

Margaret   By locking his liquor up and making him satisfy
my desire before I unlock it!

Brick   Is that what you've done, Maggie?

Margaret   Look and see. That cabinet's mighty empty
compared to before!

Brick   Well, I'll be a son of a –

*He reaches for his crutch but she beats him to it and rushes out on the
gallery, hurls the crutch over the rail and comes back in, panting.*

Margaret   And so tonight we're going to make the lie true,
and when that's done, I'll bring the liquor back here and we'll
get drunk together, here, tonight, in this place that death has
come into . . . – What do you say?

Brick   I don't say anything. I guess there's nothing to say.

Margaret   Oh, you weak people, you weak, beautiful
people! – who give up with such grace. What you want is
someone to –

She turns out the rose-silk lamp.

– take hold of you. – Gently, gently with love hand your life
back to you, like somethin' gold you let go of. I *do* love you,
Brick, I *do*!

Brick (*smiling with charming sadness*)   Wouldn't it be funny if
that was true?

The End.

Author and Director: a Delicate Situation

Whether he likes it or not, a writer for the stage must face the fact that the making of a play is, finally, a collaborative venture, and plays have rarely achieved a full-scale success without being in some manner raised above their manuscript level by the brilliant gifts of actors, directors, designers, and frequently even the seasoned theatrical instincts of their producers. I often wonder, for personal instance, if *The Glass Menagerie* might not have been a mere *succès d'estime*, snobbishly remembered by a small coterie, if Laurette Taylor had not poured into it her startling light and power, or if, without the genius of Kazan, *A Streetcar Named Desire* could have been kept on the tracks in those dangerous, fast curves it made here and there, or if the same genius was not requisite to making *Cat on a Hot Tin Roof* acceptable to a theater public which is so squeamish about a naked study of life.

A playwright's attitude toward his fellow workers goes through a cycle of three main phases. When he is just beginning in his profession, he is submissive mostly out of intimidation, for he is 'nobody' and almost everybody that he works with is 'somebody'. He is afraid to assert himself, even when demands are made on him which, complied with, might result in a distortion of his work. He will permit lines, speeches, sometimes even whole scenes to be cut from his script because a director has found them difficult to direct or an actor has found them difficult to act. He will put in or build up a scene for a star at the sacrifice of the play's just proportions and balance. A commercial producer can sometimes even bully him into softening the denouement of his play with the nearly always wrong idea that this will improve its chances at the box office. Or if he is suddenly driven to resistance, he is unable to offer it with a cool head and a tactful tongue. Intimidation having bottled him up until now, he now pops off with unnecessary violence, he flips his lid. That's the first phase of the cycle. The second is entered when the playwright has scored his first notable success. Then the dog has his day. From intimidation he passes into the opposite condition. All of a sudden he is the great, uncompromising Purist, feeling that all ideas but his own are threats to the integrity of his work. Being suddenly a 'Name' playwright, explosions of fury are no longer necessary for him to get his way. Now that he has some weight, he throws it around with the assured nonchalance of a major league pitcher warming up by the dugout. When his script is submitted to a producer by his representatives, it is not unlike the bestowal of a crown in heaven, there is a sanctified solemnity and hush about the proceedings. The tacit implication is: Here it is; take it or leave it; it will not be altered, since the slightest alteration would be nearly as sacrilegious as a revision of the Holy Scriptures.

Some playwrights are arrested at this second phase of the cycle, which is really only an aggravated reaction to the first, but sometimes the inevitable eventuality of an important failure after an important success or series of successes, will result in a moderation of the playwright's embattled ego. The temple or citadel of totally unsullied self-expression has not proven as secure a refuge as it seemed to him when he first marched triumphantly into it. It may take only one failure, it may take two or three, to persuade him that his single assessment of his work is fallible, and meanwhile, if he is not hopelessly paranoiac, he has come to learn of the existence of vitally creative minds in other departments of theater than the writing department, and that they have much to offer him, in the interpretation, the clarification, and illumination of what he has to say; and even if, sometimes, they wish him to express, or let him help them express, certain ideas and feelings of their own, he has now recognized that there are elements of the incomplete in his nature and in the work it produces. This is the third phase. There is some danger in it. There is the danger that the playwright may be as abruptly divested of confidence in his own convictions as that confidence was first born in him. He may suddenly become a sort of ventriloquist's dummy for ideas which are not his own at all. But that is a danger to which only the hack writer is exposed, and so it doesn't much matter. A serious playwright can only profit from passage into the third phase, for what he will now do is this: he will listen; he will consider; he will give a receptive attention to any creative mind that he has the good fortune to work with.

His own mind, and its tastes, will open like the gates of a city no longer under siege. He will then be willing to supplement his personal conceptions with outside conceptions which he will have learned may be creative extensions of his own.

A mature playwright who has made this third and final step in his relations to fellow workers has come to accept the collaborative nature of the theater: he knows now that each artist in the theater is able to surpass his personal limits by respect for and acceptance of the talent and vision of others. When a gifted young actor rushes up to the playwright during rehearsals and cries out, I can't feel this, this doesn't ring true to me, the writer doesn't put on the austere mask of final authority. He moves over another seat from the aisle of a rehearsal hall, and bows his head in serious reflection while the actor tells him just what about the speech or the scene offends his sense of artistic justice, and usually the writer gets something from it. If he still disagrees with the actor, he says: 'Let's get together with (whoever is directing) and talk this over at the bar next door . . . ' Maybe he won't sleep that night, but the chances are that in the morning he will re-examine the challenged segment with a sympathetic concern for an attitude which hasn't originated in his own brain and nerves, where sensibility is seated.

Now all of this that I've been rambling on about is my idea of the healthy course of development for a playwright *except* – I repeat, EXCEPT! – in those rare instances when the playwright's work is so highly individual that no one but the playwright is capable of discovering the right key for it. When this rare instance occurs, the playwright has just two alternatives. Either he must stage his play himself or he must find one particular director who has the very unusual combination of a truly creative imagination plus a true longing, or even just a true willingness, to devote his own gifts to the faithful projection of someone else's vision. This is a thing of rarity. There are very few directors who are imaginative and yet also willing to forego the willful imposition of their own ideas on a play. How can you blame them? It is all but impossibly hard for any artist to devote his gifts to the mere interpretation of the gifts of another.

He wants to leave his own special signature on whatever he works on.

Here we encounter the sadly familiar conflict between playwright and director. And just as a playwright must recognize the value of conceptions outside his own, a director of serious plays must learn to accept the fact that nobody knows a play better than the man who wrote it. The director must know that the playwright has already produced his play on the stage of his own imagination, and just as it is important for a playwright to forget certain vanities in the interest of the total creation of the stage, so must the director. I must observe that certain directors are somewhat too dedicated to the principle that all playwrights must be 'corrected'. I don't think a direcror should accept a directorial assignment without feeling that, basically, the author of the play, if it's a serious work by a playwright of ability, has earned and deserves the right to speak out, more or less freely, during the rehearsal and tryout period of the production if this can be done in a way that will not disturb the actors. Yet it sometimes happens that the playwright is made to feel a helpless bystander while his work is being prepared for Broadway. It seems to me that the director is privileged to tell the author to 'Shut up!' actually or tacitly, only when it is unmistakably evident that he, the director, is in total artistic command of the situation. Sometimes a director will go immediately from one very challenging and exhausting play production into another, being already committed by contract to do so. Then naturally he can't bring the same vitality to the second that he brought to the first. This becomes evident when the play has been blocked out, and after this blocking, little further progress is being made. The play remains at the stage of its initial blocking. The director may say, and quite honestly feel, that what he is doing is giving the public and critics a play precisely as it was written. However, this is evading the need and obligation that I mentioned first in this article, that a play must nearly always be raised above its manuscript level by the creative gifts and energies of its director, and all others involved in its production.

Perhaps it would be a good idea, sometimes, to have a good psychiatrist in attendance at the rehearsals and tryout of a difficult play, one who is used to working with highly charged creative people such as directors and actors and playwrights and producers, so that whenever there is a collision of nervous, frightened, and defensive egos, he can arbitrate among them, analyze their personal problems which have caused their professional problems, and 'smooth things over' through the clearing house of a wise and objective observer.

Once in a while the exigencies and pressures of Broadway must step aside for another set of conditions which are too fragile and spiritually important to suffer violence through the silly but sadly human conflict of egos.

The theater *can* be a maker of great friendships!

Tennessee Williams

(This essay first appeared in *Playbill*, 30 September 1957.)

Notes

10 *Great Smokies*: the Great Smokey Mountains in Tennessee were relatively cool in summer and a popular place for a holiday.

10 *Rainbow Hill*: sanitorium for alcoholics; the name suggests the popular 1940s song 'Somewhere Over the Rainbow'.

10 *AP/UP*: news wire services – Associated Press/United Press.

11 *lech*: to be sexually aroused.

12 *Books of Knowledge*: lavishly illustrated encyclopedias published by the Grolier Society in 1928 and intended for children.

13 *Spanish News*: inflated journalism associated with reporting events from the Spanish-American War, 1898; Williams's father, Cornelius Williams (CC), was a veteran of this war.

13 *Ward-Belmont*: a prestigious women's school in Nashville, Tennessee.

13 *Gayoso*: a fashionable, historic Memphis hotel; Williams's grandfather once resided there.

21 *Moon Lake*: a notorious resort, scene of gambling, prostitiution, fights, and murders, twenty miles from Clarksdale. It is referred to in several of Williams's other plays: a cock-fighting event takes place there in *Summer and Smoke* and in *Streetcar* it is where Blanche's husband Allen Grey commits suicide.

22 *Shantung*: a type of silk imported from the Shantung Province of China and used in fine, lightweight men's and women's suits.

26 *Ochsner Clinic*: New Orleans hospital founded in 1942 and widely respected for its care of cancer and heart patients. (Williams was treated there for a heart ailment in 1954.)

27 *spastic colon*: colitis.

28 *Commercial Appeal*: Memphis newspaper.

33 *redneck*: derisive name for poor Southern white farmers, synonymous with bigot.

33 *overseer*: manager responsible for running a plantation.

34 *poor as Job's turkey*: emaciated, not fed; refers to someone with no money, after the impoverished patriarch in Scripture.

34 *Vogue*: popular women's magazine on fashion.

37 *Ole Miss*: affectionate name for the University of Mississippi, located in Oxford, Faulkner's hometown, about sixty miles south of Memphis.

38 *Blackstone*: elegant Chicago hotel facing Lake Michigan.

38 *Dixie Stars*: appropriate team name since the South was the 'Land of Dixie'.

40 *sashays*: to strut or to glide, often stepping sideways to emphasise self-confidence and grace.

41 *St Paul's*: an Episcopal church by that name in Columbus, Mississippi, where Williams was born.

41 *Tiffany*: Louis Comfort Tiffany (1848–1933) was a famous American designer, stained-glass artist and maker of highly decorative glass objects.

42 *Gus Hamma*: a Delta resident, also mentioned in the one-act *Last of My Solid Gold Watches* (1945), plays poker with CC (a reference to Williams's father).

44 *old fox teeth*: treacherous.

44 *Dubonnet*: a sweet liqueur/cocktail made from wine and flavoured with spices.

44 *horsin'*: fooling, joking around.

45 *Skinamarinka-do*: children's song with this ironic stanza, given Big Daddy's inevitable voyage to the dark side of the moon: 'I love you in the morning / And in the afternoon / I love you in the evening / And underneath the moon.'

47 *Loewenstein's*: Memphis department store.

47 *Stork/Reaper*: in folklore, the stork, a gawky bird, was said to deliver babies; the Grim Reaper is a personification of death.

49 *humping*: sexual intercourse.

49 *poon-tang*: vulgar word for female genitalia; also refers to sexual intercourse.

57 *Cook's Tour*: tour of the principal places of interest. Thomas Cook founded a travel agency in the nineteenth century which arranged tours and excursions. The agency continues to this day.

58 *blue-chip stocks*: shares in solid, established companies (Standard Oil, etc.) which often cost more but were thought the safest investments.

67 *Skid Row*: poorest section of a city where transients live, often on the streets.

68 *Vicksburg tornado*: a devastating natural disaster that hit the Mississippi river town on 5 December 1953; also the basis of an influential investigative report – *The Child and His Family in Disaster: A Study of the Vicksburg Tornado.*

69 *all balled up*: to be confused, troubled, bungled or in a mess.

73 *Elks! Masons! Rotary!*: civic and quasi-religious organisations which stress the brotherhood of the members and are involved in charitable activities.

77 *hobo jungles*: large makeshift camps (tents, lean-tos) built by shiftless itinerants (hobos) who illegally stole rides aboard railroad trains during the Great Depression.

77 *Y's*: YMCAs.

78 *yellow dog freight car*: short-lived (1897–1903) Mississippi Delta Railroad, from Clarksdale to Yazoo City, known as the Yellow Dog; William C. Handy, founder of the blues, wrote a popular turn-of-the-twentieth-century song 'The Yellow Dog Blues'.

80 *pledge*: usually a college freshman who must undergo initiations before becoming a member of a fraternity. A fraternity is a social organisation of college men bonded together by tradition and ritual. Known as Greeks because their names came from Greek letters of the alphabet, fraternities had strict rules about dress codes, social events, living accommodation, etc. At the University of Missouri, Williams was a member of Alpha Tau Omega where he met fellow fraternity brother Jack Bud Pollitt, known as 'The Bull of the Ball'.

82 *shako*: bearskin cap popular in the 1930s and 1940s.

82 *moleskin*: heavy cotton fabric sheared to create a short pile on one side, like moleskin.

83 *bursitis*: inflammation, especially of elbows and knees.

84 *passing the buck*: dodging one's responsibility; US President Harry S. Truman (1945–52) had this sign on his desk – 'The Buck Stops Here'.

89 *abolition*: the abolition of slavery in 1863 in the US; the Thirteenth Amendment to US Constitution.

89 *War between the States*: US Civil War, 1861–5.

90 *hoppin' John*: a Southern dish of black-eye peas and rice, sometimes with bacon grease and chopped onions; it is a Southern custom to eat black-eye peas on New Year's Day for good luck.

92 *Friar's Point*: community near Clarksdale, also mentioned in *Summer and Smoke*.

92 *chasuble*: garment like a poncho worn by Christian priests when celebrating the Eucharist.

93 *Keeley cure*: named after an Illinois physician who used gold injections, thought to cure alcoholism.

104 *Sugar Bowl*: post-season college football game played in New Orleans to determine the best team in the Southern conference.

104 *Rose Bowl*: major US collegiate football game held in Pasadena, California, on New Year's Day.

105 *Cadillac*: one of America's most luxurious automobiles, in 1955, made by General Motors.

105 *Plantahs Bank*: Planters Bank in Memphis.

112 *belvedere*: cupola, a place to sit and look at the view.

113 *scat song*: singing nonsense syllables instead of words in jazz.

Questions for Further Study

1. There are different types of mendacity in *Cat*. Identify three or four and provide examples from the play.
2. Where do we see Maggie at her most vulnerable and at her most powerful?
3. Does Brick change at the end of the play? Provide convincing reasons why or why not.
4. Where do we see Big Daddy as kind towards Brick besides giving him a helping hand in Act Two?
5. Sports play an important role in Brick's and Skipper's lives. How do sports reflect the larger issues of the play?
6. Identify other image patterns in *Cat* besides those discussed in the Introduction.
7. Where in *Cat* do we find references to the steamy, passionate South. How does the landscape reflect/symbolise the characters and conflicts in *Cat*?
8. Big Daddy comes back briefly in the third act. Should he? If yes, what impact does he have on the ending of the play?
9. Compare and contrast *Cat* as a tragedy with another Shakespearean tragedy besides *King Lear*, for example, *Macbeth*.
10. What roles do Reverend Tooker and Dr Baugh fill in the play? How and what does Williams comment on concerning religion and medicine through these characters?
11. There are several phone calls in *Cat*. How do they fit into the play – its themes, characters, symbols?
12. Williams was accused of introducing melodrama into *Cat* – the storms, the family feud, etc. How does the play still use these dramatic techniques but transcend them at the same time?
13. Find examples of Williams's use of the Southern Gothic in *Cat*. Explain how this Williams trademark combines the lyrical with the ugly.

14. Time as the enemy is one of Williams' most persistent themes. Discuss how this theme is foregrounded in *Cat* through the characters' narratives, props, and costumes.

15. Compare and contrast Maggie with another of William's heroines, such as Blanche in *Streetcar* or the Princess in *Sweet Bird of Youth*.

16. Assume you have been asked to cast the roles of Brick, Maggie, and Big Daddy for a revival of *Cat*. Identify and justify your choice of actors you believe are best suited for these parts. Do not select actors who have previously appeared in the play.

17. Dean Shackelford has claimed that Skipper is 'the central figure' in *Cat*. Do you agree or disagree? Summon up evidence from the play to defend your decision.

18. Discuss the importance of Williams's stage directions for an interpretation of *Cat*.

19. Directors have used productions of *Cat* to make political statements (e.g., Watergate mendacity). How might the play be a reflection of current political events in your country or in the world?

20. How might *Cat* be (re)designed today to reflect an internet culture? For instance, characters using BlackBerries, Blue-rays, etc.

PHILIP C. KOLIN, University Distinguished Professor at the University of Southern Mississippi, is recognised as an international authority on the works of Tennessee Williams. He has published seven books on Williams, including *The Tennessee Williams Encyclopedia*, *Williams: A Streetcar Named Desire* for the Cambridge University Press 'Plays in Production' series, *Tennessee Williams: A Guide to Research and Performance*, and *The Influence of Tennessee Williams*. In addition, Kolin has published more than fifty scholarly articles on Williams and has served as a guest editor of four journals focusing on Williams's works. Kolin also serves on the Editorial Board of the *Tennessee Williams Annual Review*. He has also published books on Shakespeare, Edward Albee, David Rabe, Adrienne Kennedy and Suzan-Lori Parks.

Methuen Drama Student Editions

Jean Anouilh *Antigone* • John Arden *Serjeant Musgrave's Dance*
Alan Ayckbourn *Confusions* • Aphra Behn *The Rover* • Edward Bond
Lear • *Saved* • Bertolt Brecht *The Caucasian Chalk Circle* • *Fear and
Misery in the Third Reich* • *The Good Person of Szechwan* • *Life of Galileo* •
Mother Courage and her Children• *The Resistible Rise of Arturo Ui* • *The
Threepenny Opera* • Anton Chekhov *The Cherry Orchard* • *The Seagull* •
Three Sisters • *Uncle Vanya* • Caryl Churchill *Serious Money* • *Top Girls*
• Shelagh Delaney *A Taste of Honey* • Euripides *Elektra* • *Medea*•
Dario Fo *Accidental Death of an Anarchist* • Michael Frayn *Copenhagen*
• John Galsworthy *Strife* • Nikolai Gogol *The Government Inspector* •
Robert Holman *Across Oka* • Henrik Ibsen *A Doll's House* • *Ghosts*•
Hedda Gabler • Charlotte Keatley *My Mother Said I Never Should* •
Bernard Kops *Dreams of Anne Frank* • Federico García Lorca *Blood
Wedding* • *Doña Rosita the Spinster* (bilingual edition) •*The House of
Bernarda Alba* • (bilingual edition) • *Yerma* (bilingual edition)• David
Mamet *Glengarry Glen Ross* • *Oleanna* • Patrick Marber *Closer* • John
Marston *Malcontent* • Martin McDonagh *The Lieutenant of Inishmore* •
Joe Orton *Loot* • Luigi Pirandello *Six Characters in Search of an Author*
• Mark Ravenhill *Shopping and F***ing* • Willy Russell *Blood Brothers*
• *Educating Rita* • Sophocles *Antigone* • *Oedipus the King* • Wole
Soyinka *Death and the King's Horseman* • Shelagh Stephenson *The
Memory of Water* • August Strindberg *Miss Julie* • J. M. Synge *The
Playboy of the Western World* • Theatre Workshop *Oh What a Lovely
War* Timberlake Wertenbaker *Our Country's Good* • Arnold Wesker
The Merchant • Oscar Wilde *The Importance of Being Earnest* •
Tennessee Williams *A Streetcar Named Desire* • *The Glass Menagerie*

Methuen Drama Modern Classics

Jean Anouilh *Antigone* • Brendan Behan *The Hostage* • Robert Bolt *A Man for All Seasons* • Edward Bond *Saved* • Bertolt Brecht *The Caucasian Chalk Circle* • *Fear and Misery in the Third Reich* • *The Good Person of Szechwan* • *Life of Galileo* • *The Messingkauf Dialogues* • *Mother Courage and Her Children* • *Mr Puntila and His Man Matti* • *The Resistible Rise of Arturo Ui* • *Rise and Fall of the City of Mahagonny* • *The Threepenny Opera* • Jim Cartwright *Road* • *Two & Bed* • Caryl Churchill *Serious Money* • *Top Girls* • Noël Coward *Blithe Spirit* • *Hay Fever* • *Present Laughter* • *Private Lives* • *The Vortex* • Shelagh Delaney *A Taste of Honey* • Dario Fo *Accidental Death of an Anarchist* • Michael Frayn *Copenhagen* • Lorraine Hansberry *A Raisin in the Sun* • Jonathan Harvey *Beautiful Thing* • David Mamet *Glengarry Glen Ross* • *Oleanna* • *Speed-the-Plow* • Patrick Marber *Closer* • *Dealer's Choice* • Arthur Miller *Broken Glass* • Percy Mtwa, Mbongeni Ngema, Barney Simon *Woza Albert!* • Joe Orton *Entertaining Mr Sloane* • *Loot* • *What the Butler Saw* • Mark Ravenhill *Shopping and F***ing* • Willy Russell *Blood Brothers* • *Educating Rita* • *Stags and Hens* • *Our Day Out* • Jean-Paul Sartre *Crime Passionnel* • Wole Soyinka • *Death and the King's Horseman* • Theatre Workshop *Oh, What a Lovely War* • Frank Wedekind • *Spring Awakening* • Timberlake Wertenbaker *Our Country's Good*